CW0128246

THE MAYA

Jerome Martin

Illustrated by Adam Larkum
Designed by Alice Reese and Poppy Pearce

Maya consultant: Lucia R. Henderson, PhD,
Specialist in Pre-Columbian Art History
Reading consultant: Alison Kelly

Contents

3 Jungles and volcanoes
4 Stone cities
6 Towering temples
8 Lords of the Maya
10 Born to rule
12 Jungle warfare
14 Roads, ships and trade
16 What to wear
18 Eating and drinking
20 Reading and writing
22 Nights and days
24 The Maya gods
26 A Maya tale
28 Spanish invaders
30 Glossary
31 Usborne Quicklinks
32 Index

Jungles and volcanoes

The Maya are people who have lived in Mexico and Central America for thousands of years.

Long ago, they built their homes in jungles and in valleys between steep volcanoes.

The jungles were full of animals such as monkeys and jaguars.

Stone cities

This is what a Maya city might have looked like around 1,500 years ago.

Nobles and rulers lived in palaces.

Markets were held in open spaces called plazas.

Most people lived in huts with grass roofs.

Maya temples

Special courts were built for playing a ball game.

The players hit a rubber ball to and fro using only their hips and thighs.

Towering temples

Maya temples were built to look like the steep mountains where their gods lived.

This ancient temple is in the city of Tikal.

It was once brightly painted.

Ceremonies were held on a platform at the top of the temple.

Priests had to climb up lots of narrow steps.

Some rulers were buried deep inside temples.

Temples were often built to line up with the Sun or stars.

Lords of the Maya

Each Maya city had its own ruler, called the 'ajaw'. He was very powerful and wealthy.

This stone carving shows an ajaw called Shield Jaguar.

He is getting dressed for a battle.

At ceremonies, the ajaw performed special dances to please the gods.

He also had to feed the gods by piercing his body and offering them his blood.

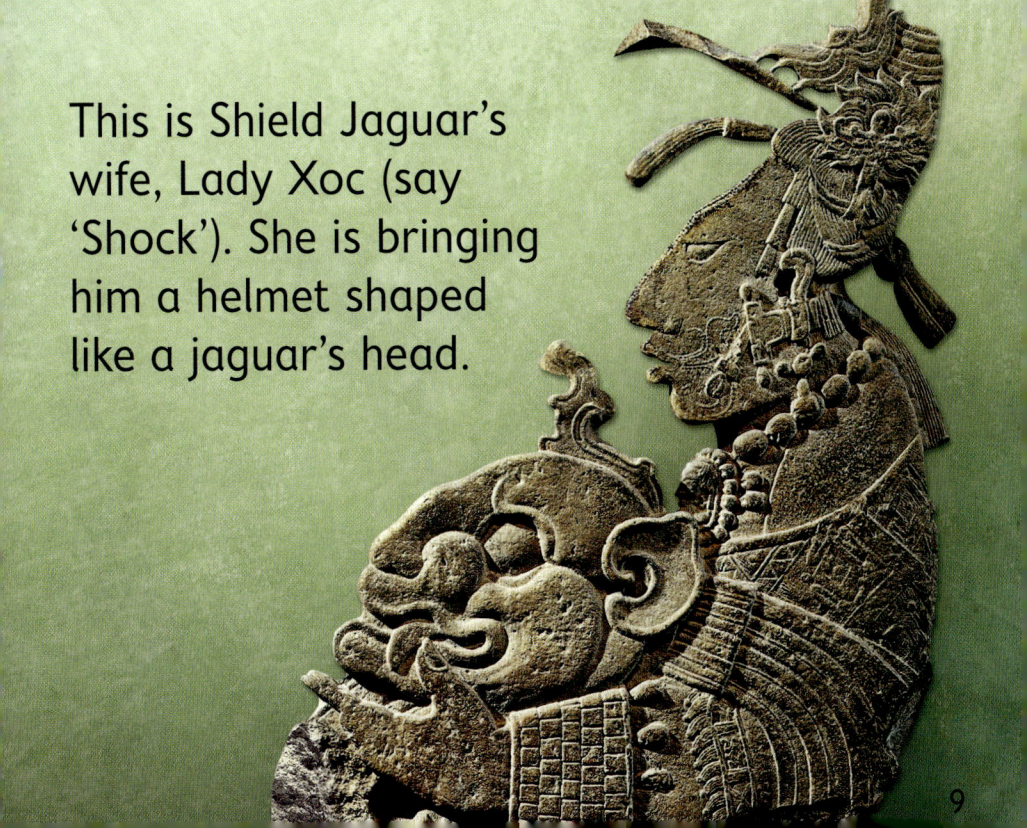

This is Shield Jaguar's wife, Lady Xoc (say 'Shock'). She is bringing him a helmet shaped like a jaguar's head.

Born to rule

Preparing for life as a noble or an ajaw began as soon as a baby was born.

Noble parents squeezed their babies' skulls between two boards. This gave their heads a tall, flat shape that people liked.

This clay figure shows a noble mother with her baby.

Noble children had their ears and lips pierced for ear flares and other ornaments.

Boys were sent away to other cities to live with great rulers and learn good manners.

When an ajaw died, his son became the new ajaw and chose a new name for himself.

A few Maya women also became powerful rulers.

Jungle warfare

Maya cities were often at war with one another.

Warriors went into battle wearing costumes and war paint.

They blew trumpets and banged drums to scare their enemies.

They fought with spears and shields and tried to capture enemy warriors.

Some prisoners became slaves. Others were killed during ceremonies.

"You can call me "He Who Captured Flaming Jaguar"."

Many ajaws added the names of famous prisoners to their own.

Roads, ships and trade

Maya traders would travel hundreds of miles to find rare goods and take them to markets to sell.

Their customers liked shells, cloth, feathers, chocolate and precious stones.

This ajaw is admiring a string of beads.

This nobleman is offering it as a gift.

Traders carried goods on their backs and walked from place to place.

Sometimes cities were connected by long, straight roads made of stone.

People carved canoes from tree trunks to transport heavy loads by sea.

Canoes could be twice as long as a modern bus.

What to wear

Clothes meant a lot to the Maya. Fine clothes and ornaments showed how important a person was.

Most women wore loose cotton dresses with bright patterns.

Most men wore a piece of material around their waists.

Both women and men put ornaments in their ears.

Ajaws and noble people wore furs, feathers and jewels.

This Maya ruler is getting dressed for a ceremony.

He is wearing a headdress with long feathers.

His ornaments are made from a green stone called jade.

A spotted jaguar skin hangs from his waist.

Some Maya filed their teeth into points, or decorated them with chips of jade.

Eating and drinking

The Maya were good farmers. They planted beans, squash and lots of corn or maize.

Maya farmers grew their vegetables in large fields dug out of the forest.

They gathered fruits such as papaya and avocado and kept bees for honey.

People caught fish, and hunted deer and pig-like animals called peccaries.

The Maya grew cacao beans and made them into many types of chocolate drinks.

These could be sweet, bitter, or spiced with hot peppers.

This clay pot once held chocolate for drinking.

They often stirred their chocolate or blew bubbles into it to make it frothy.

Reading and writing

Mayan writing was made up of pictures which stood for sounds and words.

The pictures often included animals, objects and human faces.

This writing was hard to read. Words could be spelled many different ways.

1. The Maya made paper using the bark from fig trees.

2. They pounded it flat and painted it with white plaster.

3. Scribes wrote on the paper using fine brushes.

4. They folded the paper in a zigzag to make books.

Many scribes kept their brushes in their headdresses.

21

Nights and days

The Maya studied the night sky carefully.

They learned to predict how stars and planets moved across the sky.

They wrote these movements down in calendars that measured days, months and years.

The Maya believed their calendars gave clues to what might happen each day.

Priests said which dates were lucky for holding ceremonies or even battles.

Some dates were so unlucky that people didn't work or even wash themselves.

We'll call him January 21st!

Some Maya children were named after their birthday.

The Maya gods

The Maya believed in lots of different gods and goddesses. Here are just a few.

The rain god lived in watery caves up in the mountains.

The moon goddess was often shown cuddling a rabbit.

The maize god's head looked like the top of a maize plant.

The wind god was shown playing musical instruments.

This plate shows the god of traders. He carries a heavy pack on his back.

To please the gods, the Maya danced, burned smelly tree sap and offered them gifts of food.

A Maya tale

Maya legends tell of two magical boys, the Hero Twins, who grew up in the forest with their lazy, bullying half-brothers.

The twins had to fetch wood and carry water for their brothers.

They were miserable until one day they came up with a clever trick...

The twins talked their half-brothers into climbing a tree in the forest.

Magically, the tree began to grow.

The bullies were soon stuck on a narrow branch high in the air.

Twist your clothes into tails to balance better!

In a flash, the tails grew hair and the two bullies turned into noisy monkeys.

Spanish invaders

About 500 years ago, people from Spain came to take over the Maya's lands.

Spanish soldiers attacked and captured the Maya's cities, towns and villages.

Many Maya died in the battles, or from illnesses they caught from the Spanish.

The Spanish burned Mayan books and tried to wipe out the Maya's way of life.

Over time, the ruins of their great cities were covered up by trees and vines.

Although they left their ancient cities, many Maya people still live in Mexico and Central America today.

Glossary

Here are some of the words in this book you might not know. This page tells you what they mean.

jaguar - a large jungle cat. Its fur has yellow and black spots.

noble - a rich person. Nobles wore special clothes and precious jewels.

ajaw - say 'ah-haw'. The ruler of a Maya city.

ear flare - an ornament that Maya men and women wore in their ears.

headdress - a showy head covering worn by nobles and rulers.

cacao beans - seeds that can be used to make chocolate.

scribe - a person whose job it was to write and copy words in books.

Usborne Quicklinks

Would you like to find out more about the Maya? You can visit Usborne Quicklinks for links to websites with amazing facts, photographs, and even a video of a ball game.

Go to **usborne.com/Quicklinks** and type in the keywords "**beginners maya**". Make sure you ask a grown-up before going online.

Notes for grown-ups

Please read the internet safety guidelines at Usborne Quicklinks with your child. Children should be supervised online. The websites are regularly reviewed and the links at Usborne Quicklinks are updated. However, Usborne Publishing is not responsible and does not accept liability for the content or availability of any website other than its own.

This statue shows a Maya ball game player. He is wearing a large belt to protect his body from the hard rubber ball.

Index

ball games, 5
battles, 8, 12-13, 23, 28
books, 20-21, 22-23, 28, 30
cacao, 19, 30
ceremonies, 7, 9, 13, 17, 23
cities, 4-5, 8, 11, 12, 15, 28-29, 30, 31
clothes, 8, 9, 12, 16-17, 27, 30, 31
ear flares, 11, 30
feathers, 14, 16, 17
food, 9, 14, 18-19, 24, 25, 30

gods, 6, 9, 24-25
headdresses, 17, 21, 30
jaguars, 3, 8-9, 13, 17, 30
jungle, 3, 12-13, 18, 26, 29, 30
monkeys, 3, 27
names, 8-9, 11, 13, 23
nobles, 4, 10-11, 14, 16, 30
ornaments, 11, 14, 16, 17, 30
rulers, 4, 7, 8-9, 10-11, 13, 14, 16-17, 30
scribes, 21, 30
stars, 7, 22
temples, 5, 6-7
traders, 14-15, 25

Acknowledgements

Photographic manipulation by John Russell
Additional design by Katie Webb

Photo credits

The publishers are grateful to the following for permission to reproduce material:
cover © Kenneth Garrett/Danita Delimont/Alamy Stock Photo; **p1** © travelstock.ca/Alamy Stock Photo;
p6 © age fotostock/Alamy Stock Photo; **p8-9** © De Agostini Picture Library/G. Dagli Orti/Bridgeman Images;
p10 © Justin Kerr, Mayavase.com; **p14** © Justin Kerr, Mayavase.com; **p17** © De Agostini Picture Library/G. Dagli Orti/Bridgeman Images; **p19** © Museo de Arqueologia, Guatemala/Jean-Pierre Courau/Bridgeman Images;
p20 © Museo de America, Madrid, Spain/Bridgeman Images; **p25** © Justin Kerr, Mayavase.com;
p29 © Kelly Cheng/Getty Images; **p31** © World History Archive/Alamy Stock Photo.

Every effort has been made to trace and acknowledge ownership of copyright. If any rights have been omitted, the publishers offer to rectify this in any subsequent editions following notification.

This edition first published in 2021 by Usborne Publishing Ltd., Usborne House, 83-85 Saffron Hill, London EC1N 8RT, England. usborne.com Copyright © 2021, 2018 Usborne Publishing Ltd. All rights reserved. The name Usborne and the Balloon logo are Trade Marks of Usborne Publishing Ltd. No part of this publication may be reproduced, stored in a retrieval system, or transmitted in any form or by any means without the prior permission of Usborne Publishing Ltd. U.E.

ROMANS

Katie Daynes

Illustrated by Adam Larkum
Designed by Katrina Fearn

Romans consultant: Aude Doody, PhD, University College Dublin
Reading consultant: Alison Kelly

Contents

- 3 In Roman times
- 4 People of Rome
- 6 At home
- 8 On the streets
- 10 What to wear
- 12 Going shopping
- 14 Farming
- 16 Banquets
- 18 At the baths
- 20 Gods and goddesses
- 22 Building power
- 24 At school
- 26 In the army
- 28 Games and races
- 30 Glossary
- 31 Usborne Quicklinks
- 32 Index

In Roman times

The first Romans lived in the city of Rome over a thousand years ago. They had a strong army and took over many countries.

Every Roman town had a big open space where people met, heard the latest news and went shopping.

People of Rome

In Rome, there were rich people, poor people and slaves. The most powerful person was the emperor.

The emperor ruled over all Roman lands.

Men called senators gave him advice.

This coin shows the head of Augustus, the first emperor.

He won many battles and made Rome more peaceful.

People captured in a battle were often sold as slaves.

Rich Romans bought slaves to do hard work for them.

Some masters made their slaves work in their storerooms.

Other masters made their slaves cook meals for them.

Once a year, slaves and masters changed places for the day.

5

At home

In Roman towns, most people rented rooms. Only rich Romans could afford houses.

Poor people rented rooms on the top floor.

Richer people had big rooms lower down.

There were often shops at street level.

Romans didn't use wallpaper. They just painted pictures on their walls.

This is a Roman wall painting of a villa. Villas were big houses where the rich lived.

Rich Romans had mosaics on their floors.

A worker spread plaster on the floor.

He made a pattern out of small tiles.

On the streets

The streets of Rome were often packed with people. Vehicles were only allowed at night.

At dawn, street cleaners swept the streets and sellers arrived with their goods.

By noon, the streets were very busy. Rich Romans were carried in boxes called litters.

At night, the vehicles arrived. People carried torches because there were no street lights.

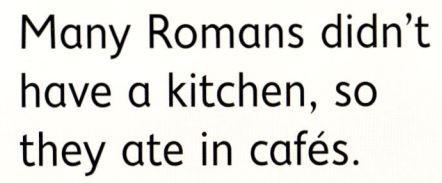

Many Romans didn't have a kitchen, so they ate in cafés.

They got their drinking water from public fountains.

This mosaic shows musicians playing to people on the street.

What to wear

Most Roman men and women dressed up in long, flowing pieces of material.

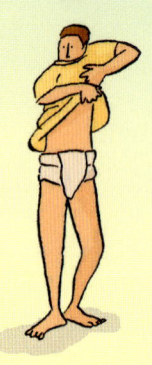

Everyone wore a simple cloth tunic.

Women wore a dress over their tunic.

Sometimes they wore a big shawl too.

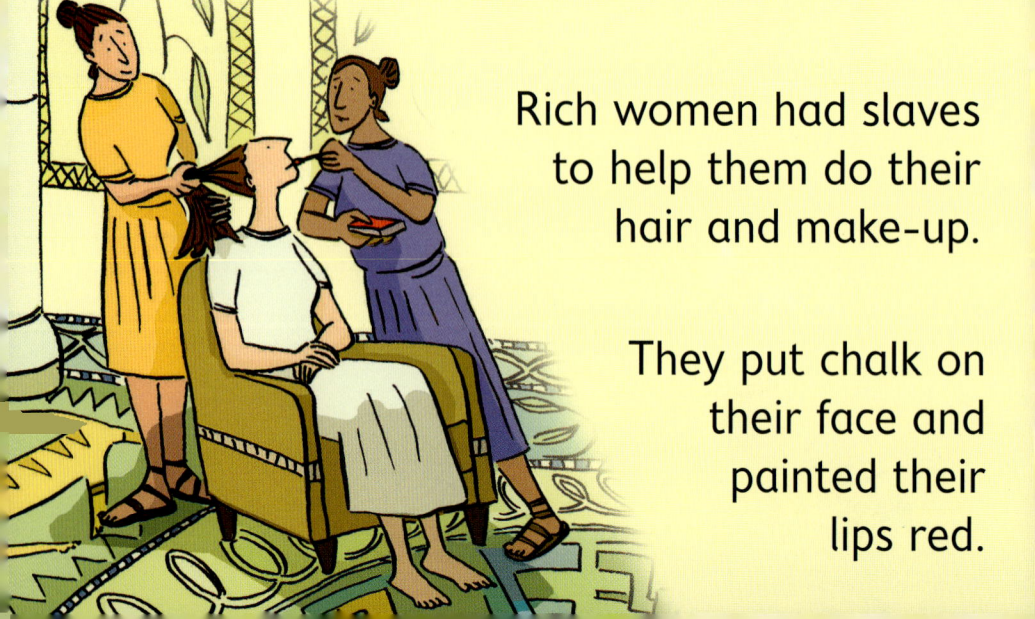

Rich women had slaves to help them do their hair and make-up.

They put chalk on their face and painted their lips red.

Important men draped a huge piece of material over their tunic. It was called a toga.

This is a statue of a Roman man wearing a toga.

Only the emperor was allowed to dress all in purple.

Going shopping

People did their shopping in local shops or at a market.

This shop sold olive oil.

This one sold material.

People bought pottery here.

Food sellers made fresh food each day at the back of their shops.

Bakers ground wheat to make flour.

They made dough with the flour...

...then baked the dough to make bread.

This carving shows a butcher chopping meat in his shop.

At the markets, people sold fresh fruit and vegetables from the countryside.

Farming

Most Roman food came from farms.

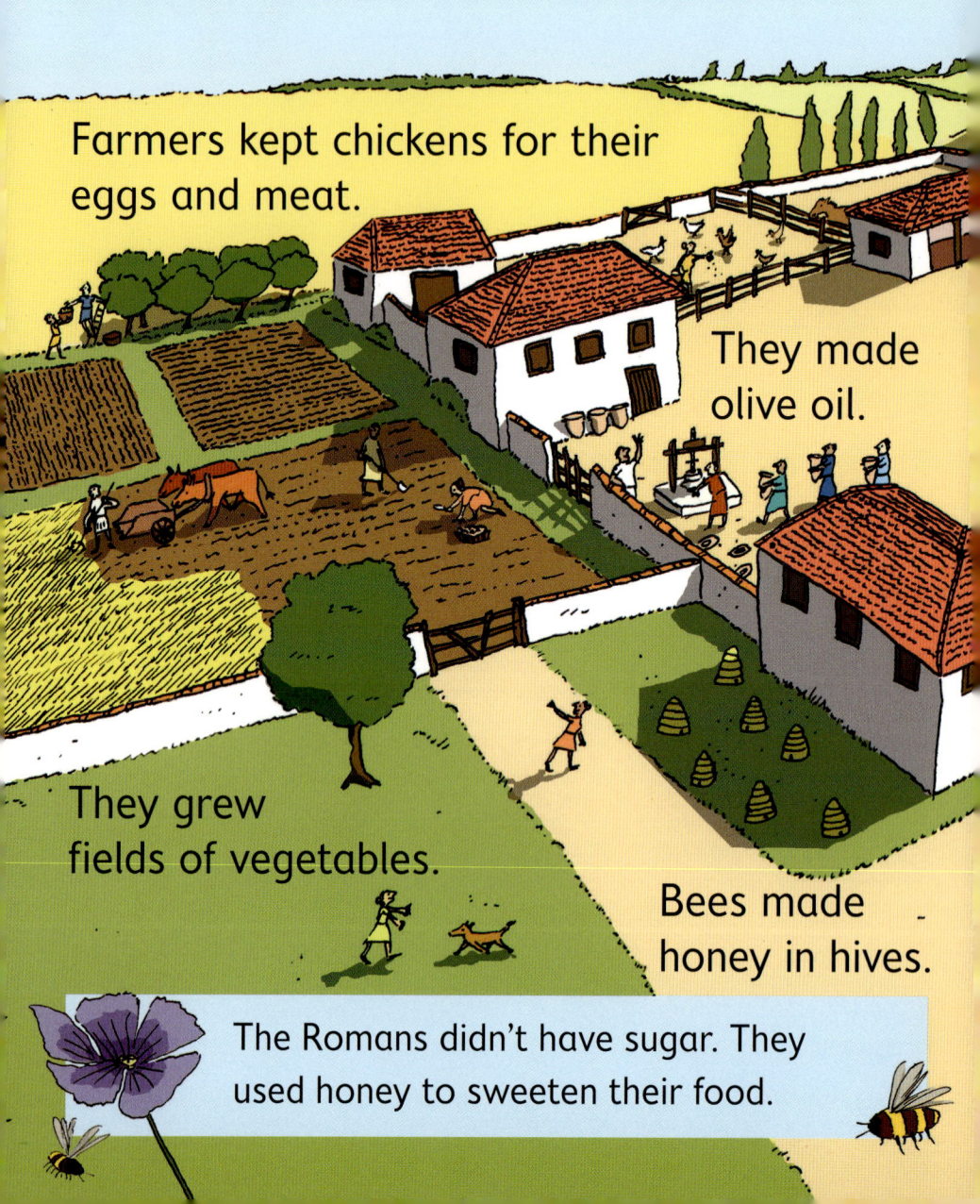

Farmers kept chickens for their eggs and meat.

They made olive oil.

They grew fields of vegetables.

Bees made honey in hives.

The Romans didn't have sugar. They used honey to sweeten their food.

Sheep were kept for their milk, wool and meat.

Pig meat was very popular.

Farmers grew grapes to make juice and wine.

They picked the grapes...

...squashed out the juice...

...and stored it in jars.

Banquets

Rich people invited friends to huge evening meals called banquets.

Guests arrived and took their sandals off by the door.

Slaves washed their feet, then led them to the banquet room.

The guests lay down on couches and had their hands washed.

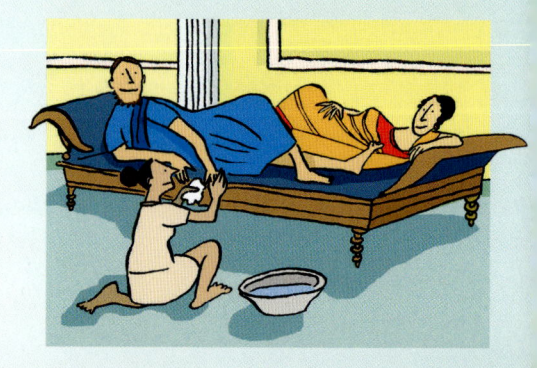

Slaves brought in fancy foods and lots of wine.

Guests ate with their fingers, straight from the serving plates.

They were entertained with music and dancing.

Stuffed dormice and peacock brains were served as treats.

At the baths

In Roman times, people didn't wash at home. They went to the public baths.

First they went into the steam room.

Then they soaked in the hot room.

They relaxed in the warm room...

...before a dip in the cold pool outside.

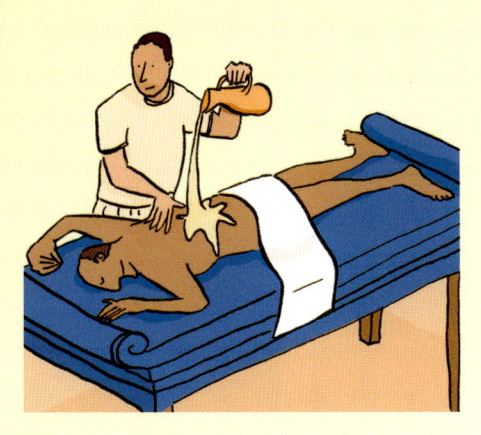

Romans washed with oil. Slaves rubbed it onto their skin.

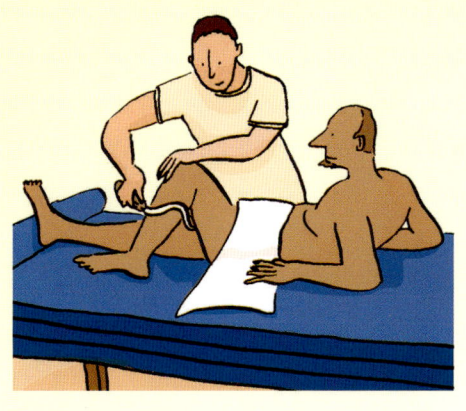

Then they scraped it off with a stick. The dirt came off too.

Roman public toilets looked like this. People sat in a line on the holes.

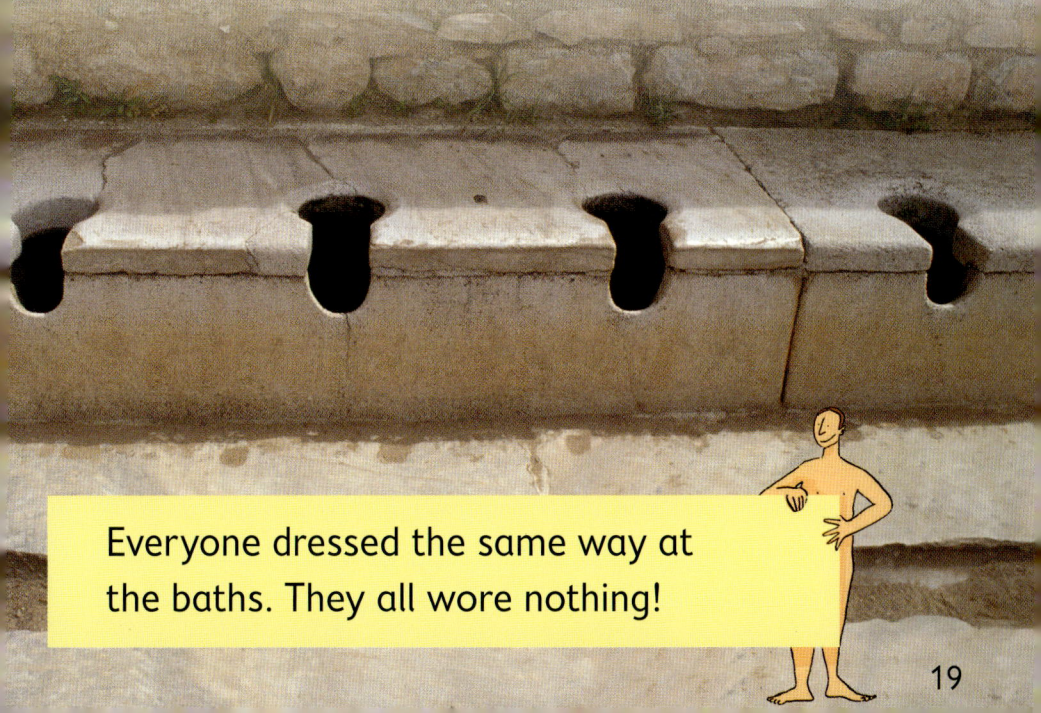

Everyone dressed the same way at the baths. They all wore nothing!

Gods and goddesses

The Romans used to worship gods and goddesses. Here are some important ones.

Jupiter was the king of the gods.

He married the powerful goddess Juno.

Their son, Mars, was god of war.

Diana was the goddess of hunting.

Mercury took messages for Jupiter.

Venus was the goddess of love.

On holy days, people went to temples with gifts for the gods.

Priests killed animals for the gods. Then they ate the meat.

Some Roman temples still stand today. This one is missing its roof.

Every spring, the Romans had a party to celebrate Flora, the goddess of flowers.

Building power

The Romans built many amazing things, such as temples, ships and aqueducts.

Aqueducts were bridges that carried water into towns. Their arches were hard to build.

Builders made a curved wood frame.

They built bricks around the frame.

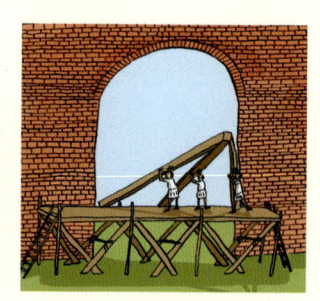

Then they took the frame away.

The Romans built sailing ships to collect food and material from other countries.

They also built fast ships for sea battles. Men attacked their enemies with balls of fire.

Inside the ships, men sat in rows and pulled on oars to make the ship go faster.

At school

Only the sons of rich Romans went to school in Roman times.

They were taught to read and write.

They used a metal pen to scratch words onto a wax tablet.

Then they smoothed the wax and tried writing again.

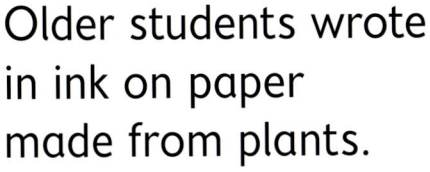

Older students wrote in ink on paper made from plants.

They wrote speeches and learned how to act them out.

All students learned how to count. Romans wrote numbers using letters, like this.

1 = I   5 = V   9 = IX
2 = II   6 = VI   10 = X
3 = III   7 = VII   11 = XI
4 = IV   8 = VIII   12 = XII

Girls didn't go to school. They got married at a very young age.

In the army

The Romans had a very powerful army made up of thousands of soldiers.

The soldiers spent days marching to new battles.

Each evening, they built a camp where they could rest.

They broke through the wall around their enemy's town.

Then they marched in, using their shields like a tortoise's shell.

Roman soldiers looked like this when they went into battle.

Games and races

For a fun day out, Romans went to the games or to the races.

The games took place in a big round stadium.

The day began with music, dancing and circus tricks.

Then slaves called gladiators fought each other.

Many gladiators were killed in fights at the games.

Sometimes there were animal hunts at the games too. This Roman wall painting shows a man hunting a lion.

At chariot races, men rode in carts pulled by horses.

They raced around a track. It was very fast and dangerous.

Glossary

Here are some of the words in this book you might not know. This page tells you what they mean.

emperor – the man who ruled over Rome and all Roman lands.

slave – a person who works for no money. Rich Romans owned slaves.

mosaic – a picture or pattern on the floor made of little stones or tiles.

litter – a big box for rich Romans to travel in. They were carried by slaves.

aqueduct – a bridge built to carry drinking water into a Roman town.

gladiator – a man who had to fight at the games. He was usually a slave.

chariot – a cart pulled by two, four, six or sometimes even eight horses.

Usborne Quicklinks

Would you like to find out more about the ancient Romans? Visit Usborne Quicklinks for links to websites with videos, facts and activities about life in Roman times.

Go to **usborne.com/Quicklinks** and type in the keywords "**beginners romans**". Make sure you ask a grown-up before going online.

Notes for grown-ups

Please read the internet safety guidelines at Usborne Quicklinks with your child. Children should be supervised online. The websites are regularly reviewed and the links at Usborne Quicklinks are updated. However, Usborne Publishing is not responsible and does not accept liability for the content or availability of any website other than its own.

This is a painting of the goddess Flora. It shows her picking flowers.

Index

aqueducts 22, 30
banquets 16-17
baths 18-19
battles 4, 5, 23, 26, 27
chariots 29, 30
clothes 10-11
dancing 17, 28
drink 9, 15, 17
emperor 4, 11, 30
farming 14-15
food 5, 9, 12, 13, 14, 15, 16, 17, 21
gladiators 28, 30
gods and goddesses 20-21, 31

homes 6-7
litters 8, 30
mosaics 7, 9, 30
music 9, 17, 28
painting 6, 7, 29
Rome 3, 4, 30
school 24-25
ships 23
shopping 3, 6, 12-13
slaves 4, 5, 10, 16, 17, 19, 28, 30
soldiers 26, 27
temples 21
togas 11
toilets 19

Acknowledgements

Photographic manipulation by Emma Julings

Photo credits

The publishers are grateful to the following for permission to reproduce material: **cover** © fotoVoyager/Getty Images; **p1** © Corbis/Gianni Dagli Orti; **p4** © The Trustees of The British Museum; **p7** © Corbis/Mimmo Jodice; **p9** © Corbis/The Art Archive; **p11** © Corbis/Araldo de Luca; **p13** © Corbis/The Gallery Collection; **p19** © Robert Harding/Michael Jenner; **p21** © Alamy/Frank Miesnikowicz; **p22** © Corbis/Free Agents Ltd; **p26-27** © Corbis/Charles & Josette Lenars; **p29** © Corbis/Vanni Archive; **p31** © Corbis/Mimmo Jodice.

Every effort has been made to trace and acknowledge ownership of copyright. If any rights have been omitted, the publishers offer to rectify this in any subsequent editions following notification.

This edition first published in 2021 by Usborne Publishing Ltd., 83-85 Saffron Hill, London EC1N 8RT, England. usborne.com Copyright © 2021, 2015, 2004 Usborne Publishing Ltd. All rights reserved. The name Usborne and the Balloon logo are Trade Marks of Usborne Publishing Ltd. No part of this publication may be reproduced, stored in a retrieval system, or transmitted in any form or by any means without the prior permission of Usborne Publishing Ltd. UE.

VIKINGS

Stephanie Turnbull

Designed by Laura Parker and Hanri Van Wyk
Illustrated by Adam Larkum

Viking consultant: Dr. Richard Hall
Reading consultant: Alison Kelly

Contents

- 3   Viking life
- 4   Different Vikings
- 6   At home
- 8   A trip to town
- 10   What to wear
- 12   Gods and goddesses
- 14   At a feast
- 16   Fun and games
- 18   Viking boats
- 20   Wild warriors
- 22   Attack!
- 24   Exploring
- 26   Famous Vikings
- 28   A Viking funeral
- 30   Glossary
- 31   Usborne Quicklinks
- 32   Index

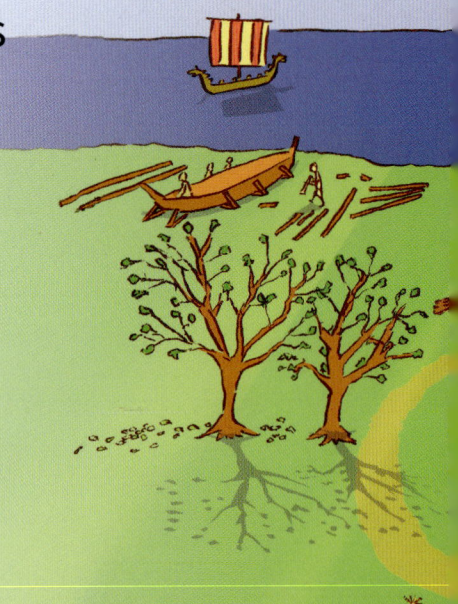

Viking life

The Vikings were people who lived in Denmark, Norway and Sweden more than a thousand years ago.

Most Vikings lived on small farms in the countryside.

Different Vikings

The richest Vikings were kings and jarls, and the poorest people were thralls. Most ordinary Vikings were farmers.

Kings ruled over large areas of land called kingdoms.

Jarls were important leaders who owned lots of land.

Some ordinary Vikings worked as fishermen or traders.

Thralls were slaves who had to work for richer Vikings.

All Viking men except thralls trained to fight as warriors.

This statue shows a jarl ready to go into battle.

Many Vikings had nicknames, such as Thorkell the Tall and Eric Bloodaxe.

At home

Viking families lived in wooden or stone buildings called longhouses. There was one big room inside.

The walls of this longhouse have been removed so you can see inside.

Clothes, tools and weapons were stored in big chests or hung up on pegs.

A fire was used for cooking food and heating the room.

At one end of the longhouse was a stable for animals.

People slept on benches around the sides of the room.

Toilets were holes dug outside, often in small huts.

7

A trip to town

There were a few big Viking towns where people went to buy and sell goods.

Traders sold silk, spices and glass from faraway lands.

Blacksmiths shaped hot metal into tools and weapons.

People walked on paths made out of wooden planks.

Towns were noisy, crowded places, with animals everywhere.

People often paid for goods with coins like these, or pieces of silver from bracelets and rings.

What to wear

Vikings wore thick clothes that kept them warm when it was very cold.

Women and girls had long dresses made of wool.

A shorter dress went on top, held in place with two brooches.

Men and boys wore leggings, tunics and leather belts.

Everyone had leather shoes and cloaks of wool or fur.

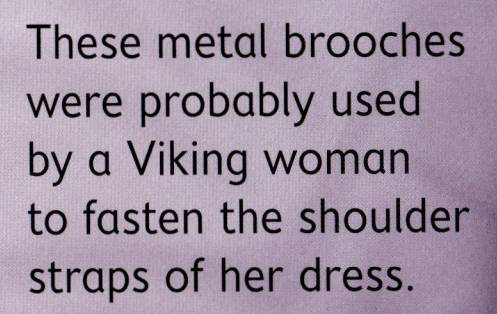

These metal brooches were probably used by a Viking woman to fasten the shoulder straps of her dress.

All Vikings had long hair, which they often tied out of the way.

Gods and goddesses

Vikings believed that a rainbow bridge led to a world above them called Asgard. Many gods and goddesses lived there.

This painting is about 300 years old. It shows Heimdall, a god who guarded the rainbow bridge.

Vikings thought that a giant snake circled the human world.

Odin, the king of the gods, rode an eight-legged horse.

Freya, the goddess of love, could turn herself into a falcon.

Thor was the god of thunder. He carried a magic hammer.

Loki was half-god and half-giant. He played cruel tricks on the gods.

At a feast

Vikings loved having feasts to celebrate weddings, winning wars and other events.

Thralls cooked lots of food. They roasted meat and fish over a fire and made stews.

Guests sat at long wooden tables to eat. They drank out of hollow cows' horns.

Musicians played and poets called skalds told exciting stories of battles and heroes.

There was no sugar in Viking times, but food was sweetened with honey instead.

These wooden bowls and spoons were once used by Vikings. Now they are old and cracked.

Fun and games

Vikings spent their free time playing games, repairing weapons and making beautiful things.

Some people made lucky charms like this one. It shows Thor holding his magic hammer.

Many Vikings enjoyed skiing and skating in the winter.

Sometimes men had wrestling contests or sword fights.

They showed off their strength by lifting huge rocks.

Vikings also enjoyed hunting with spears and arrows.

17

Viking boats

The Vikings were good sailors, and they made all kinds of boats. The biggest boats were called longships.

This modern boat has been built to look similar to a Viking longship.

When Vikings sailed to war they hung their shields on the side of the boat, like this.

Long planks of wood were nailed together to make the bottom and sides of the boat.

A wide deck was added, as well as a mast for a big, square sail and holes for oars.

A dragon's head was often carved at the front of a longship to scare enemies.

Wild warriors

All Viking men owned weapons and were quick to use them against their enemies.

They wore thick leather or metal helmets.

This is a copy of a Viking helmet with eye holes and a nose guard.

A few extra-fierce, bloodthirsty warriors called themselves Berserks.

Vikings wore padded clothes for battles. Rich men had tunics made of metal rings.

They fought with swords, axes or spears. Swords were carried in a holder.

All fighters carried large wooden shields. Some men painted their shields.

21

Attack!

Many Vikings were poor, so they sometimes sailed to England and raided places there.

Vikings often attacked early in the morning, taking people by surprise.

They captured or killed anyone who got in their way.

Raiders set buildings on fire to force out the terrified people.

They grabbed all the money and treasure they could find.

23

Exploring

Vikings began to raid towns all over Europe. Many of them found good land for farming and decided to live there.

Vikings also settled in Iceland and Greenland. They hunted fish, whales and seals to eat.

Some Vikings sailed as far as North America and tried to set up farms there.

They were often attacked by Native Americans, so they soon decided to leave.

The first person to sail to North America was Leif the Lucky.

Viking traders went as far as Asia to buy and sell goods.

This modern tapestry shows Leif the Lucky standing at the front of his longship.

Famous Vikings

The Vikings loved to tell thrilling stories about brave heroes from the past. Some of these stories might not be true.

Olaf was a king who drowned himself after losing a battle. The man jumping overboard in this painting may be Olaf.

Ragnar Hairy-Breeches was a terrifying king who once raided Paris.

Erik the Red was a fearless warrior and adventurer who explored Greenland.

Erik the Red's daughter Freydis was a skilled sailor who fought in battles.

Harald Hardrada was a clever leader who once dug a tunnel into an enemy castle.

A Viking funeral

Ordinary Vikings were buried in simple graves when they died, but important people had magnificent funerals.

Sometimes a person was placed in a boat with their belongings.

The boat was set on fire and everything was burned.

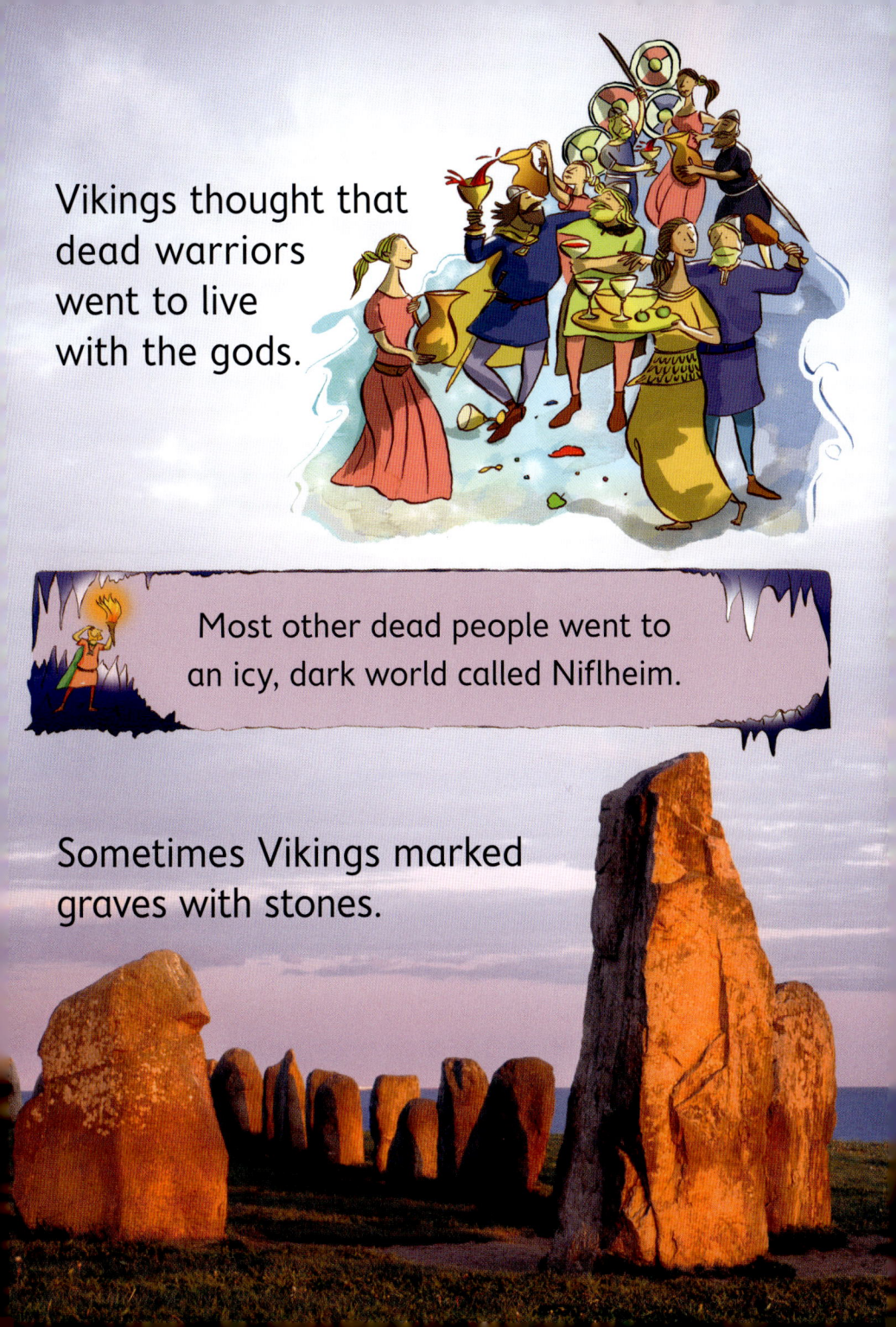

Vikings thought that dead warriors went to live with the gods.

Most other dead people went to an icy, dark world called Niflheim.

Sometimes Vikings marked graves with stones.

Glossary

Here are some of the words in this book you might not know. This page tells you what they mean.

trader - a Viking who bought and sold goods, often from other countries.

longhouse - a large building where a Viking family lived.

tunic - a long-sleeved top that was worn with a belt.

skald - a poet who told Viking poems and long stories called sagas.

longship - a long Viking boat used by warriors or explorers.

raid - to make a surprise attack. Some Vikings raided towns and villages.

Native Americans - the first people to live in North America.

Usborne Quicklinks

Would you like to find out more about the Vikings? Visit Usborne Quicklinks for links to websites with videos, facts and activities about the Vikings – farmers, warriors and explorers.

Go to **usborne.com/Quicklinks** and type in the keywords "**beginners vikings**". Make sure you ask a grown-up before going online.

Notes for grown-ups

Please read the internet safety guidelines at Usborne Quicklinks with your child. Children should be supervised online. The websites are regularly reviewed and the links at Usborne Quicklinks are updated. However, Usborne Publishing is not responsible and does not accept liability for the content or availability of any website other than its own.

This dragon's head carving was found in a Viking ship.

Index

boats, 4, 18-19, 22, 24, 25, 28
clothes, 6, 10, 21
death, 28-29
Erik the Red, 27
explorers, 24-25, 27
farms, 3, 24
food, 7, 14, 15, 24
Freydis, 27
gods and goddesses, 12-13, 16, 29
Greenland, 24, 27
Harald Hardrada, 27
helmets, 20
hunting, 17, 24
Iceland, 24
jarls, 4, 5
kings, 4, 13, 26, 27
Leif the Lucky, 25
longhouses, 6-7, 30
longships, 18-19, 25, 30
money, 9, 23
North America, 24, 25
Olaf, King, 26
Ragnar Hairy-Breeches, 27
raiding, 22-23, 24, 27, 30
shields, 18, 21
skalds, 14, 30
thralls, 4, 14
traders, 4, 8, 25, 30
warriors, 5, 20-21, 29
weapons, 6, 8, 16, 17, 20, 21

Acknowledgements

Photographic manipulation by Nick Wakeford

Photo credits

The publishers are grateful to the following for permission to reproduce material: **cover** © helmet, from the Vendel Treasure, Uppland, c.600AD (metal), Vendel Period/Historiska Museet; Stockholm, Sweden/Bridgeman Images; **p1** © Adam Woolfitt/Corbis; **p5** © Macduff Everton/Corbis; **p9** © Werner Forman/Corbis; **p11** © The Trustees of the British Museum; **p12** © Arni Magnusson Institute/Bridgeman Art Library; **p15** © York Archaeological Trust; **p16** © Werner Forman/Corbis; **p18** © Kai Gjessing/Mjosen-lange.no; **p20** © Medieval Reproductions; **p25** © The Jamestown-Yorktown Foundation/Bridgeman Art Library; **p26** © Private Collection/Bridgeman Art Library; **p28-29** © Jon Arnold Images/Alamy; **p31** © Werner Forman/Corbis.

Every effort has been made to trace and acknowledge ownership of copyright. If any rights have been omitted, the publishers offer to rectify this in any subsequent editions following notification.

This edition first published in 2021 by Usborne Publishing Ltd., Usborne House, 83-85 Saffron Hill, London EC1N 8RT, England. usborne.com Copyright © 2021, 2015, 2006 Usborne Publishing Ltd. All rights reserved. The name Usborne and the Balloon logo are Trade Marks of Usborne Publishing Ltd. No part of this publication may be reproduced, stored in a retrieval system, or transmitted in any form or by any means without the prior permission of Usborne Publishing Ltd. UE.

Castles

Stephanie Turnbull

Designed by Laura Parker
Illustrated by Colin King

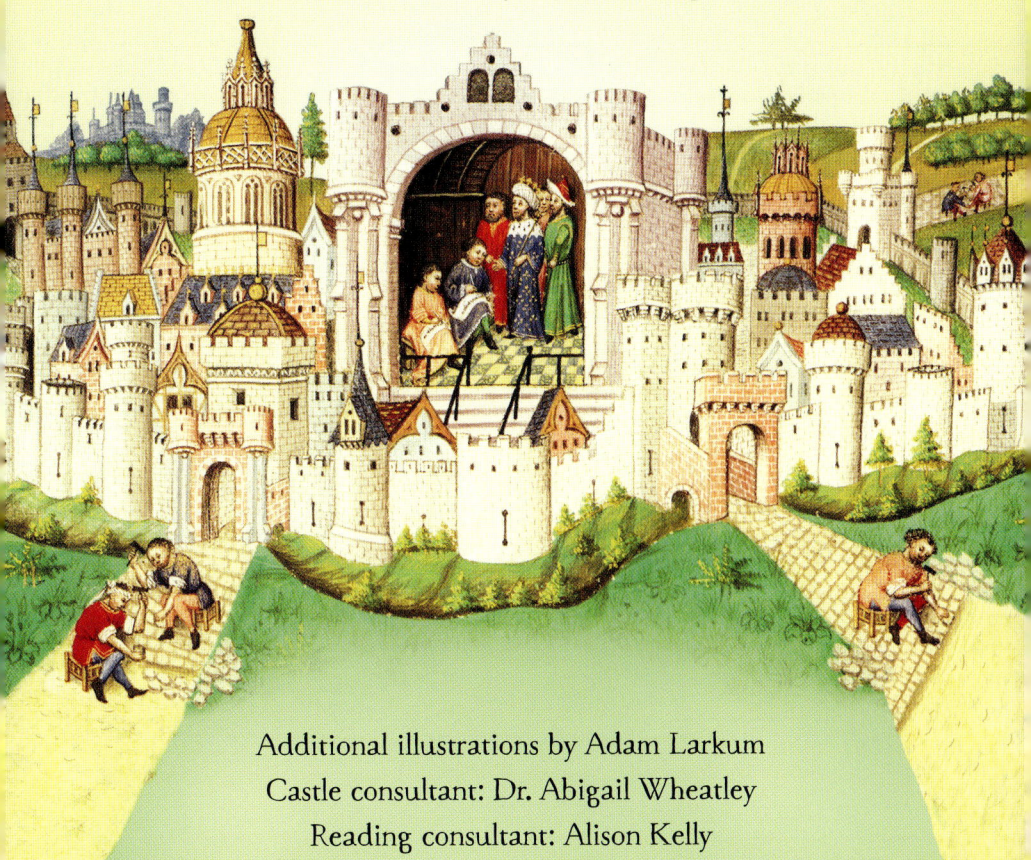

Additional illustrations by Adam Larkum
Castle consultant: Dr. Abigail Wheatley
Reading consultant: Alison Kelly

Contents

- 3 High on a hill
- 4 A huge home
- 6 Types of castles
- 8 The keep
- 10 Castle life
- 12 Fun and games
- 14 Hunting
- 16 In the kitchen
- 18 Fabulous feasts
- 20 Knights
- 22 At a joust
- 24 Attack!
- 26 Fighting back
- 28 Castles in ruins
- 30 Glossary
- 31 Usborne Quicklinks
- 32 Index

High on a hill

The ruins of a huge stone castle stand on a hill. Hundreds of years ago, this castle was full of people.

Some castles were built on cliffs, so they had a good view out to sea.

A huge home

Castles were built for rich people such as lords and ladies or kings and queens.

Servants worked and lived in the castle grounds.

Soldiers guarded the castle gate.

The castle's main tower is called a keep.

A thick wall was built to keep enemies out.

Rich people had two or three castles. If they were tired of one, they moved to another.

5

Types of castles

Some castles were made of wood. The keep was built on a high mound of earth.

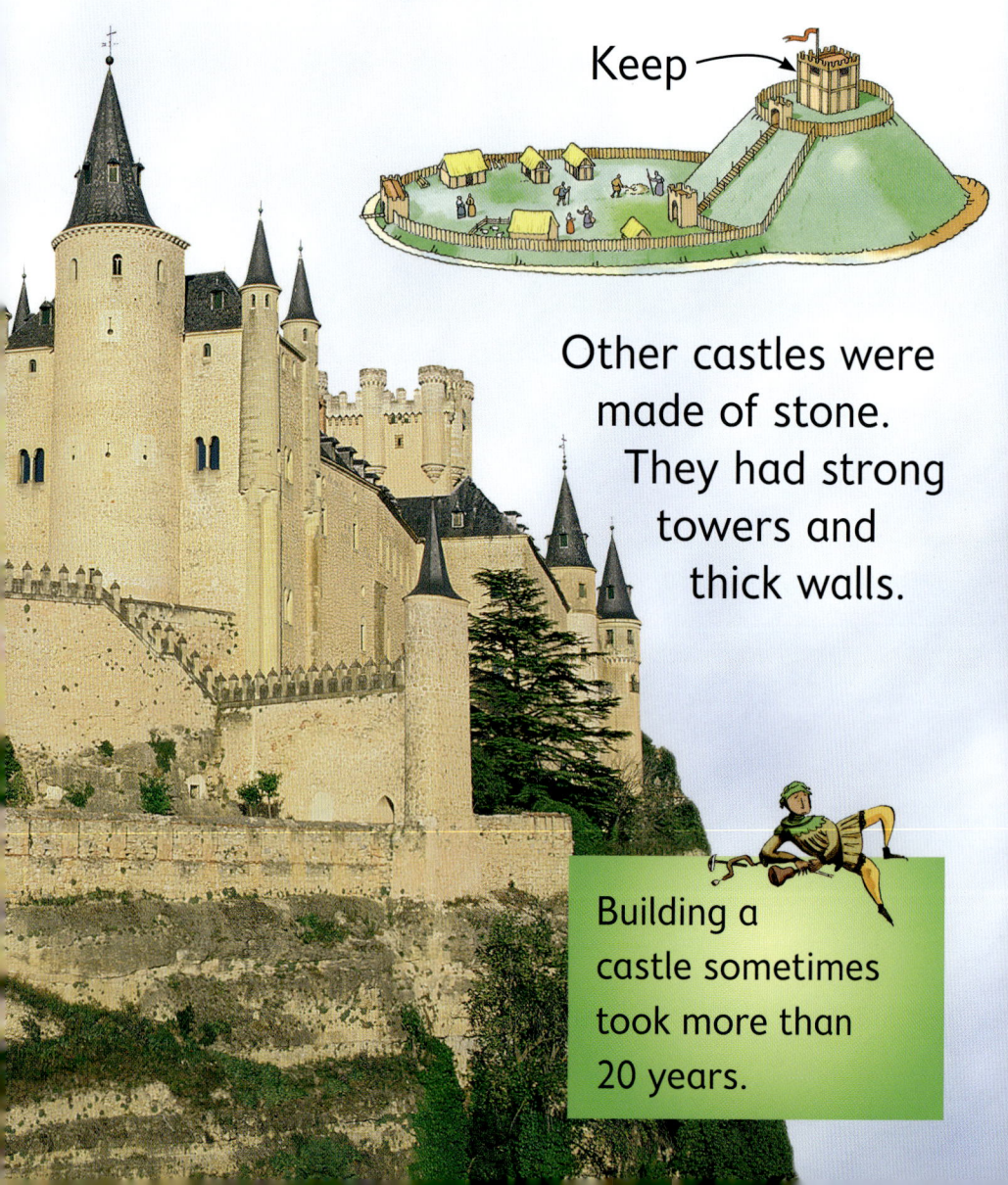

Keep

Other castles were made of stone. They had strong towers and thick walls.

Building a castle sometimes took more than 20 years.

Some castles had water around them. This is called a moat. The moat helped to keep out enemies.

People crossed the moat on a wooden platform called a drawbridge.

The drawbridge was pulled up with chains if an enemy came near.

The keep

There were lots of rooms inside the keep. The best rooms belonged to the lord and his family.

A bedroom

Great Hall

Chapel

Guard room

Storeroom

A castle toilet was just a hole in the floor. Underneath was a chute that led to a pit outside.

Castles were always full of rats. Can you spot ten rats in the keep?

Castle life

Castle owners lived in comfortable rooms. They slept in big, soft beds like this red one.

Curtains around the bed kept them snug and warm.

Servants had to sleep on the hard, cold floor.

People in castles got up early. Sometimes a bell was rung at dawn to wake everyone.

Stone castles could be damp and chilly. Huge fires helped to keep rooms warm.

People had baths in big wooden tubs. Servants heated the water over a fire.

Castles were noisy places. Servants worked, children played games and dogs barked.

11

Fun and games

There were no televisions in castle times. People had to find other things to do.

Acrobats often visited castles to put on shows.

Jugglers juggled balls or hoops.

Musicians sang songs and played instruments.

Many castles had a jester. His job was to tell jokes and make everyone laugh.

This picture was painted about 700 years ago. It shows a group of musicians playing tunes for a king.

Hunting

Lords and ladies enjoyed hunting. Birds called falcons were trained to hunt. Here are four stages of training a falcon.

1. The falcon got used to being carried and fed.

2. It was kept on a rope, and flew after bits of food.

3. Later, the falcon was able to fly freely.

4. It killed small birds and came back to its owner.

A hood helped to keep the falcon calm when it was taken out to be trained.

It was very fashionable to own a falcon. People took them everywhere.

In the kitchen

The kitchen was a building in the castle grounds. All the meals were made there.

Meat was roasted over a fire, on a stick called a spit.

This is how part of a castle kitchen might have looked.

1. To bake bread, bakers lit a fire in an oven to heat it up.

2. They mixed dough for bread and made it into loaves.

3. The loaves went in the oven when the fire died down.

4. The oven was still hot, so the bread soon cooked.

Castles didn't have refrigerators, so food went bad quickly. Cooks added spices to disguise the horrible taste.

Fabulous feasts

Huge meals called feasts were served in the Great Hall of the castle.

Important guests sat at a high table.

Everyone else sat on long benches.

There were no forks in castle times. People usually ate with their fingers.

People ate lots of meat and fish.

Cooks decorated food with feathers and fruit.

Amazing models made of sugar and paper were carried in to impress the guests.

Knights

Knights were rich, important soldiers. They helped to protect castles against enemies.

Knights had shapes or pictures on their shields. Each knight had his own pattern.

First a knight put on a thick, padded vest.

Over this he wore a shirt made of metal.

Metal plates covered his arms, legs and chest.

Then he put on a long top and big gloves.

He wore a heavy metal helmet on his head.

He carried a wooden shield to protect him.

At a joust

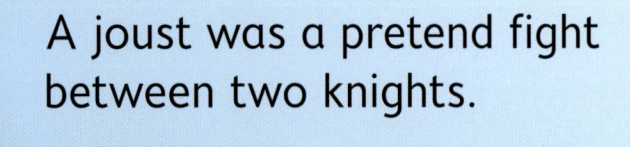

A joust was a pretend fight between two knights.

The knights held long poles called lances.

They rode on strong horses called chargers.

The winner of a joust got a prize. Sometimes he won the losing knight's horse and weapons.

The two knights charged up to each other, on a narrow track.

Each knight tried to hit the other one on the shield with his lance.

The knight who was able to stay on his horse was the winner.

Attack!

Sometimes castles were attacked. Enemies often used a machine called a trebuchet.

Lever

1. Soldiers pulled a big lever back.

2. They loaded the end with rocks.

3. Then they let the lever spring up.

4. The rocks hit the castle walls.

Enemies used trebuchets to throw dead animals into castles, to spread diseases.

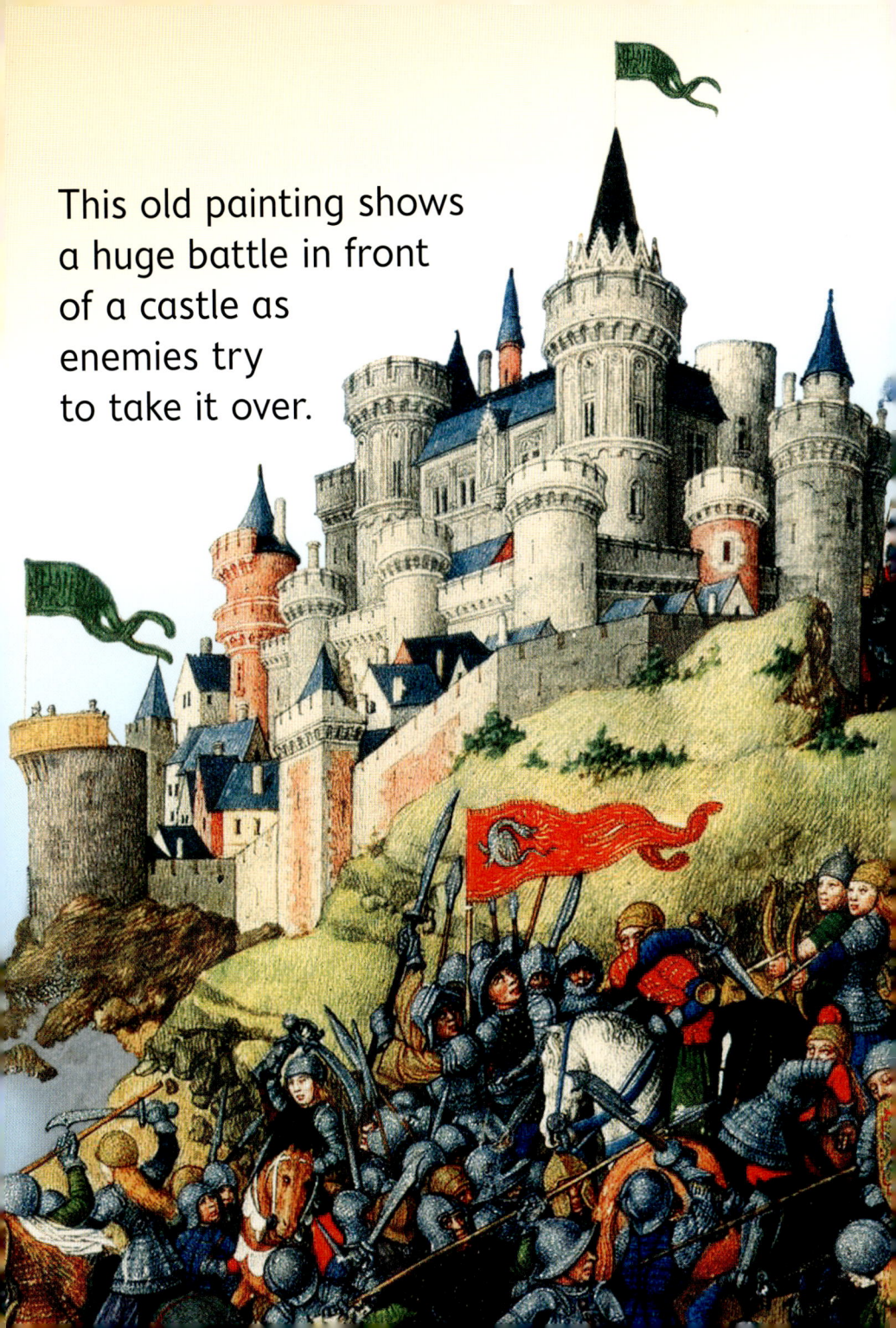

This old painting shows a huge battle in front of a castle as enemies try to take it over.

Fighting back

Soldiers tried to keep their castle safe from enemies.

They dropped rocks or boiling water onto the heads of enemies who came near.

Sometimes enemies tried to sneak into castles in disguise.

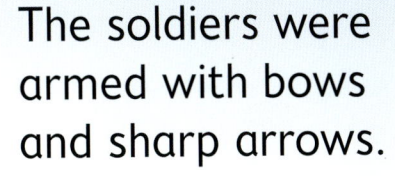

The soldiers were armed with bows and sharp arrows.

They fired arrows through thin slits in the wall.

This castle has many arrow slits in its walls. Soldiers also shot arrows from the roof.

Castles in ruins

Most castles are now empty. They have crumbled over the years.

This is how Raglan Castle, in Wales, might have looked 400 years ago.

This is how the castle looks now.

Some castles were destroyed by enemies in attacks.

This tower was blown up, but part of it still stands.

A few castles have been rebuilt for people to live in.

Glossary

Here are some of the words in this book you might not know. This page tells you what they mean.

keep - the main tower of a castle. It usually had a wall around it.

drawbridge - a bridge that was pulled up to keep enemies out of a castle.

falcon - a type of large bird. Falcons can be trained to hunt smaller birds.

feast - a huge meal for lots of people, with plenty to eat and drink.

shield - a tough, wooden plate. Knights used shields to protect themselves.

joust - a game where two knights tried to knock each other off their horses.

trebuchet - a machine that could fling rocks and other things through the air.

Usborne Quicklinks

Would you like to find out more about castles? You can visit Usborne Quicklinks for links to websites with videos, amazing facts and things to make and do.

Go to **usborne.com/Quicklinks** and type in the keywords "**beginners castles**". Make sure you ask a grown-up before going online.

Notes for grown-ups

Please read the internet safety guidelines at Usborne Quicklinks with your child. Children should be supervised online. The websites are regularly reviewed and the links at Usborne Quicklinks are updated. However, Usborne Publishing is not responsible and does not accept liability for the content or availability of any website other than its own.

Neuschwanstein Castle was built for a German king, but he died before it was finished.

Index

acrobats, 12
bedrooms, 8, 10
bows and arrows, 27
chapel, 8
drawbridge, 7, 30
falcons, 14-15, 30
feasts, 18-19, 30
fighting, 24-25, 26-27, 29
food, 9, 16, 17, 18, 19
Great Hall, 8, 18
guard room, 9
hunting, 14-15
jesters, 12
jousts, 22-23, 30

jugglers, 12
keep, 5, 6, 8-9, 30
kitchen, 16-17
knights, 20-21, 22-23
moat, 7
musicians, 12, 13
rats, 9
ruined castles, 28-29
servants, 4, 10, 11
shields, 20, 21, 30
soldiers, 4, 24, 25, 26, 27
storeroom, 9
trebuchet, 24, 30
wooden castles, 6

Acknowledgements

Photographic manipulation by Emma Julings
With thanks to Grace Bryan-Brown and The National Trust for the model on page 19.

Photo credits
The publishers are grateful to the following for permission to reproduce material:
cover © Tim Gartside/Robert Harding Picture Library; **p1** © The Bridgeman Art Library/Bibliothèque Royale de Belgique, Brussels, Belgium; **p2-3** © Photononstop/Superstock; **p6** © Gary Cralle/Getty Images; **p7** © Mike Morton/E & E Picture Library; **p10** © Leeds Castle (Angelo Hornak); **p13** © Lebrecht Collection; **p15** © Yann Arthus-Bertrand/Corbis; **p16** Crown copyright: Historic Royal Palaces; **p20** Crown Copyright CADW: Welsh Historic Monuments; **p22** © Pete Dancs/Getty Images; **p25** © Historic Picture Archive/Corbis; **p27** © Araldo de Luca/Corbis; **p28** © Chris Bland; Eye Ubiquitous/Corbis; **p29** © English Heritage Photo Library; **p31** © Ric Ergenbright/Corbis.

Every effort has been made to trace and acknowledge ownership of copyright. If any rights have been omitted, the publishers offer to rectify this in any subsequent editions following notification.

This edition first published in 2021 by Usborne Publishing Ltd., Usborne House, 83-85 Saffron Hill, London EC1N 8RT, England. usborne.com Copyright © 2021, 2015, 2006, 2003 Usborne Publishing Ltd. All rights reserved. The name Usborne and the Balloon logo are Trade Marks of Usborne Publishing Ltd. No part of this publication may be reproduced, stored in a retrieval system, or transmitted in any form or by any means without the prior permission of Usborne Publishing Ltd. U.E.

Digging up the past

Lisa Jane Gillespie

Designed by Sam Chandler
and Josephine Thompson

Illustrated by Maria Cristina Pritelli

Archaeology consultant: Dr. Tony Pollard, University of Glasgow
Reading consultant: Alison Kelly

Contents

3 Hidden history
4 Signs and clues
6 Dig in
8 Palaces and huts
10 Ancient people
12 A buried town
14 Art from long ago
16 Underwater past
18 Ancient tombs
20 War stories
22 Standing tall
24 What's the date?
26 Model buildings
28 Preserving the past
30 Glossary
31 Usborne Quicklinks
32 Index

People who dig things up to learn about the past are called archaeologists (say *ark-ee-ol-o-jists*). You'll find out more about them in this book.

Hidden history

Things from long ago sometimes get buried underground. Slowly, layers of soil build up over them and plants or buildings cover them.

Ancient things, like these jewels, help experts to understand how people lived in the past.

Signs and clues

Archaeologists look for different clues that tell them where something might be buried.

Lumps and bumps on the ground can mark where old buildings once stood. These grassy bumps show where an old fortress used to be.

Old coins or pieces of tile can be washed up by rivers. This may mean more are buried nearby.

Ancient pots are sometimes found in fields. Experts search the area to try to find more.

Everyday objects such as tools can be found buried near ruins and old buildings.

Sometimes machines such as metal detectors are used to help to find things underground.

Beep!

Dig in

Archaeologists only begin to dig when they think they know where something is buried.

1. Often, they use shovels to remove the top layer of soil.

2. They use trowels to search through the soil very carefully.

3. If they find something fragile, they brush it clean.

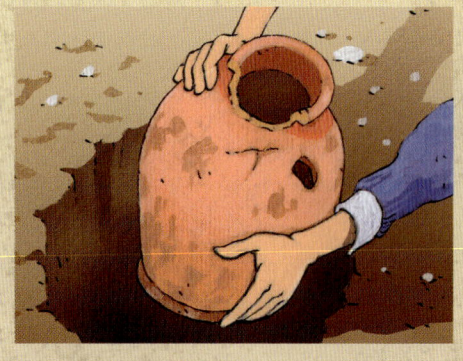

4. Then they take it away to preserve and study it.

This archaeologist has dug up the bones of someone who died long ago. She is cleaning them with a soft brush.

Palaces and huts

Buried buildings can give many clues about what life was like in the past.

This ancient palace was dug up in Greece. It belonged to a rich king and had hundreds of rooms with beautiful paintings on the walls.

Thousands of years ago, people in Europe lived in simple round huts. The remains of some of them have been dug up.

The remains helped experts to find out how ancient people built the huts. First, they dug lots of holes and stood wooden posts in them.

Then, they made a wall from sticks and mud. They used poles to make a frame for the roof. They covered this with straw.

Ancient people

Sometimes the remains of ancient people and clothes are dug up. Experts study them to find out how people looked long ago.

In 1991, a man's body was found frozen in ice on a mountain in Italy.

Scientists did lots of tests on the body. They discovered it was 5,000 years old.

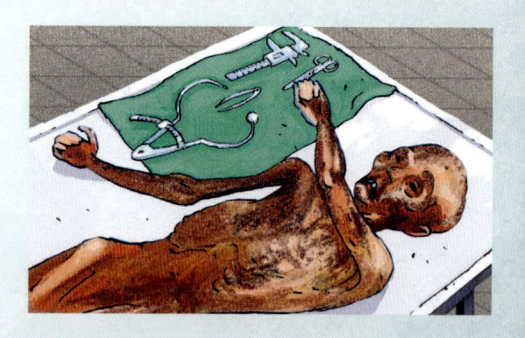

This is what the man might have looked like, when he was alive.

Archaeologists can find out what a person's face looked like, just by studying a skull.

These leather shoes were found in mud near a river. They are 600 years old.

Old shoes and clothes show what people liked to wear in the past.

A buried town

The ancient Roman town of Pompeii in Italy was buried in ash 2,000 years ago when a volcano exploded. Thousands of people died.

All the ruins in this photograph were dug up. They have helped experts to find out what the town was like.

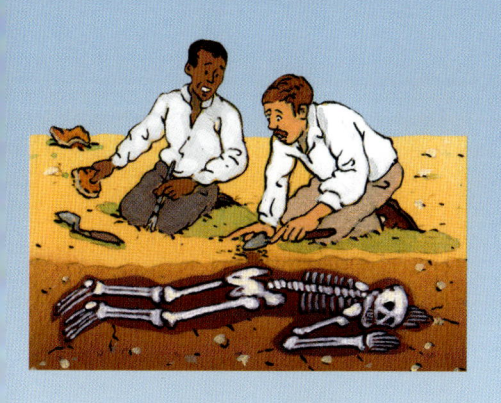

There were holes in the hardened ash where bodies had rotted away.

Archaeologists carefully poured plaster into the holes left by the bodies.

When the plaster set hard, they broke away the ash and dug up the plaster shape.

Some unbroken eggs were even found preserved in the ash.

Art from long ago

Sometimes archaeologists dig up ancient jewels, carvings and paintings. In 2009, these gold and silver ornaments were found in a field in England.

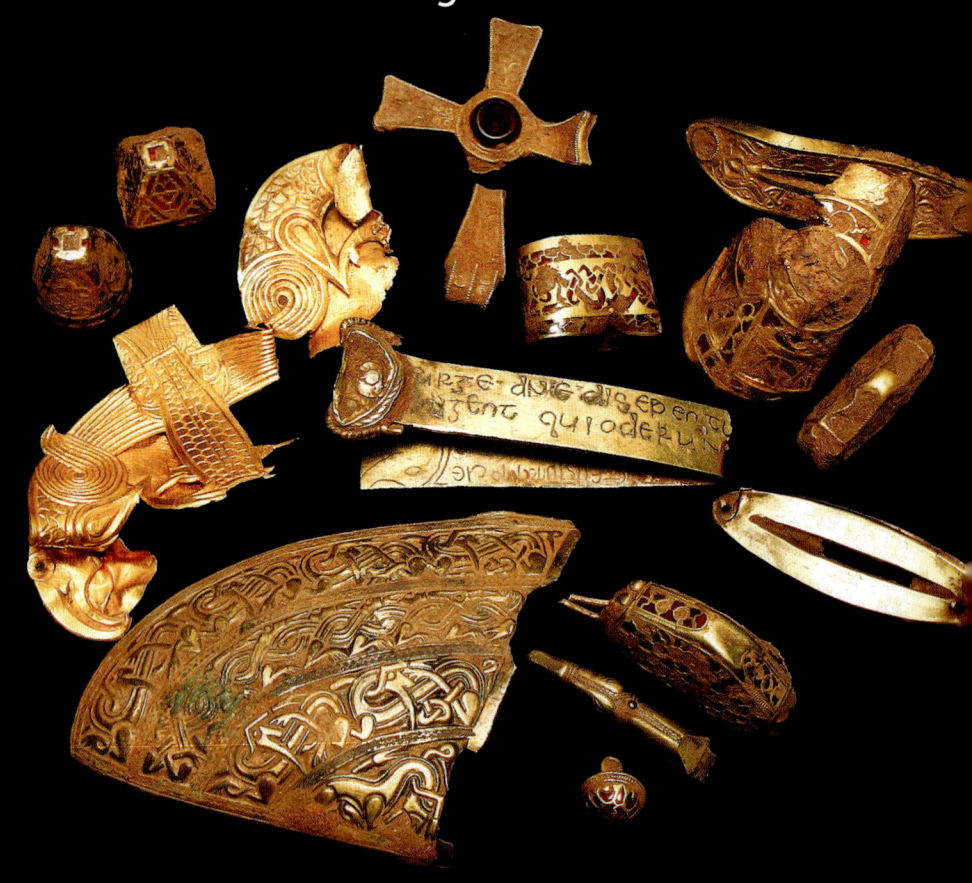

Experts think someone buried them around a thousand years ago, to keep them safe.

This 500 year old mask is from Mexico. It's made from shells and turquoise stones and shows the face of a god.

In Australia there are some rock paintings of kangaroos that are 20,000 years old.

Underwater past

Things from the past are sometimes found at the bottom of rivers, lakes or oceans.

These divers are studying pots from a shipwreck off the coast of Turkey. The pots contained wine.

1. A ship called the Mary Rose sank in 1545. Divers found it 340 years later.

2. Experts carefully tied the remains of the ship to a huge metal frame.

3. They attached cables to the frame and lifted the ship out of the water.

4. The divers found lots of cannons and weapons beside the shipwreck, too.

Sometimes mini submarines are used to explore shipwrecks.

Ancient tombs

In the past, many dead people were buried in tombs. Sometimes, amazing things were buried with them.

These statues are known as the Terracotta Army. They were discovered in the tomb of a Chinese emperor who died 2,000 years ago.

In 1922, a tomb was discovered buried under sand in the desert in Egypt.

The tomb was full of statues and treasure. It belonged to a king called Tutankhamun.

This golden coffin was found deep in the tomb. It is decorated to show Tutankhamun's face and jewels.

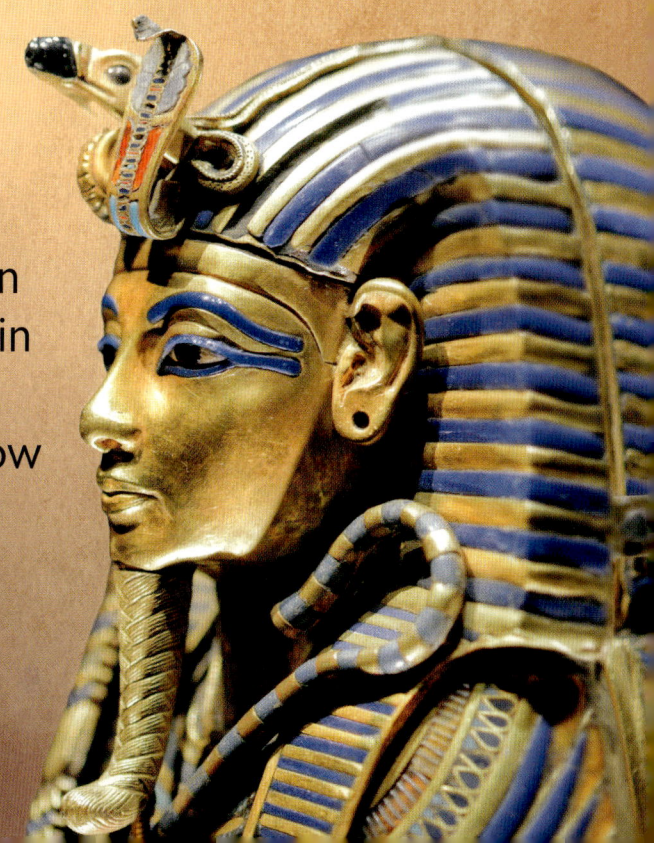

War stories

Some archaeologists try to find out about wars that were fought in the past. They dig on battlefields and look for old weapons.

Divers found this plane in the Pacific Ocean. It crashed during an air battle in World War II.

A team of experts dug at Little Bighorn, USA, where a famous battle was fought in 1876.

They found bullets, arrowheads and bones, and marked where each thing was found.

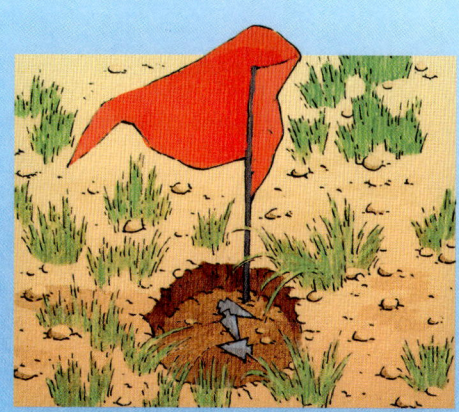

This helped them to find out what happened during the battle.

Standing tall

Some amazing buildings and statues from the past were never buried.

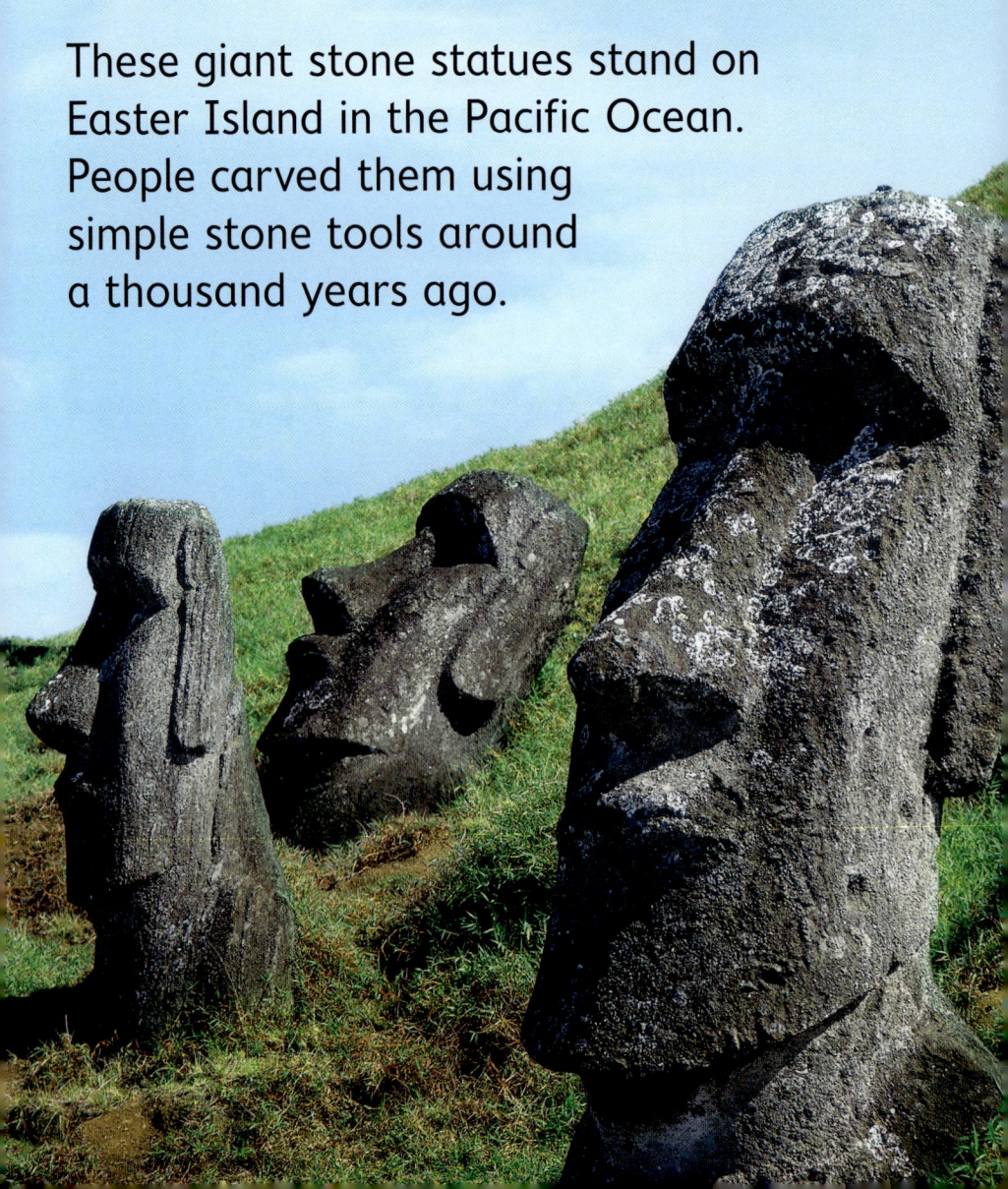

These giant stone statues stand on Easter Island in the Pacific Ocean. People carved them using simple stone tools around a thousand years ago.

1. The pyramids in Egypt are huge tombs where ancient kings were buried.

2. Each pyramid was made from thousands of huge stone blocks.

3. Teams of workers pulled the blocks into position using wooden sleds.

4. As a pyramid grew, the workers dragged the blocks up ramps made from sand.

Long ago, no one knew how huge stones were moved in ancient times. Some people thought giants lifted them.

What's the date?

Archaeologists have lots of ways of finding out the age of the things they dig up.

Some things, such as coins, have the year they were made stamped on them.

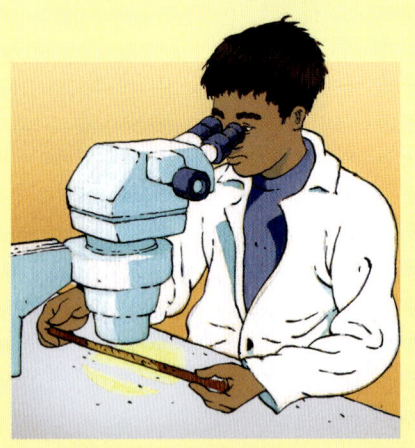

Scientific tests can tell the age of things made from some natural materials, such as wood.

If the age of one object is known, it's likely that other things of the same style are the same age.

Sometimes lots of things are buried in the same place. Usually, the deeper the things are buried, the older they are.

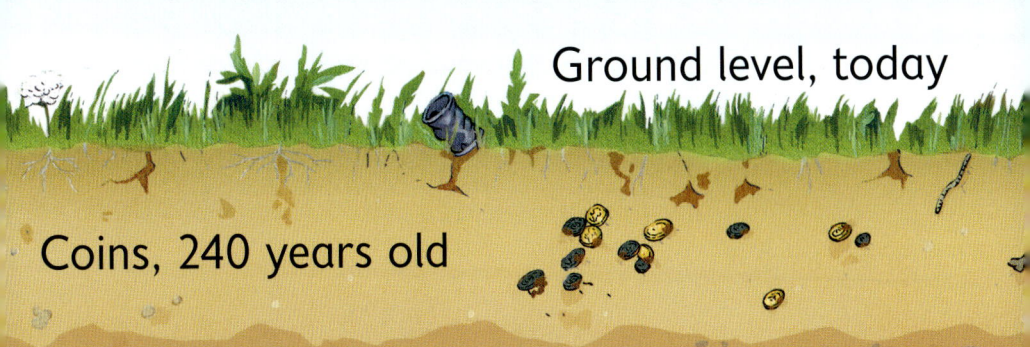

Ground level, today

Coins, 240 years old

Floor tiles, 700 years old

Remains of a wall, 900 years old

Jug, 1,800 years old

Iron sword, 2,200 years old

Model buildings

Sometimes experts use computers to make models of ancient buildings. This helps archaeologists to find out more about them.

1. The remains of the buildings are measured and photographed.

2. All the photos and measurements are carefully entered into a computer.

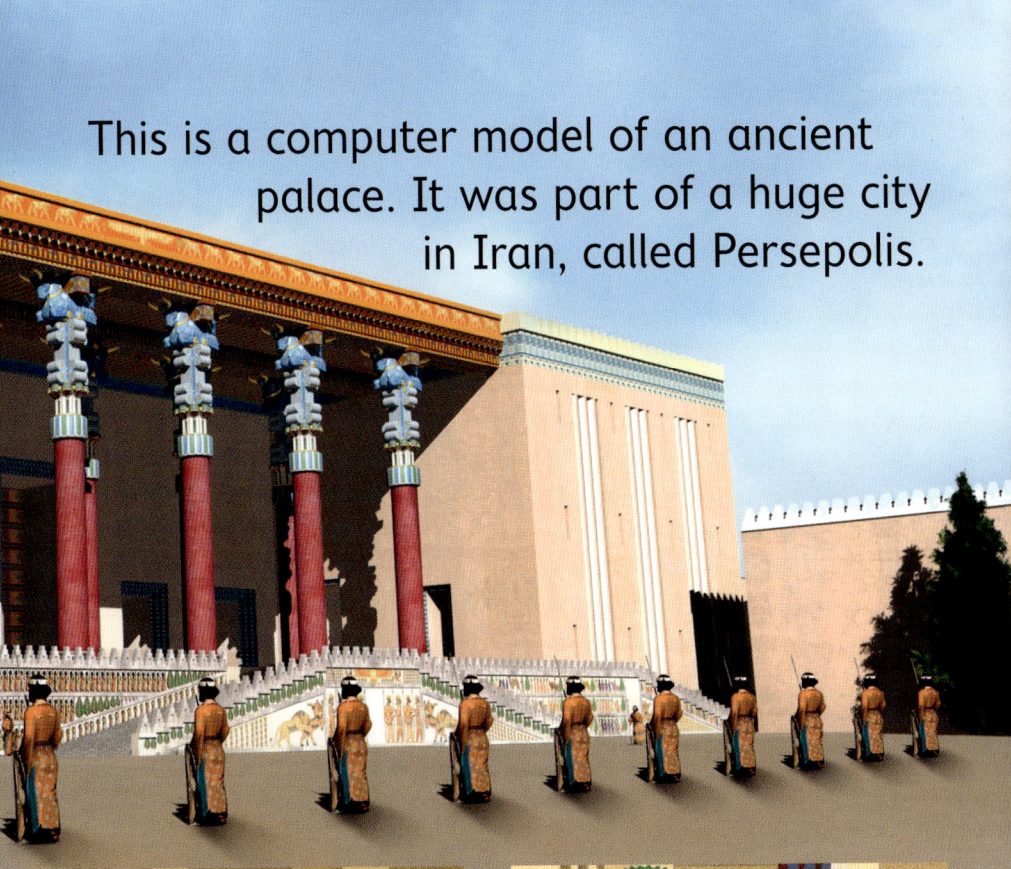

This is a computer model of an ancient palace. It was part of a huge city in Iran, called Persepolis.

3. Then experts use a program to turn the information into a model on screen.

4. They add details to show what the place looked like when it was newly built.

Preserving the past

Things that have been buried for hundreds of years are often fragile or broken. Experts take care of them, to stop them from falling apart.

Archaeologists in England found pieces of wood with Roman writing on them.

Experts cleaned the pieces carefully and stuck some of them back together.

The wood was a party invitation, sent by a Roman lady to her friend.

This ancient metal helmet was rebuilt from hundreds of tiny pieces. It is now on display in a museum for visitors to see.

Some ancient statues can never be put back together. Their noses, heads or arms have never been found.

Glossary

Here are some of the words in this book you might not know. This page tells you what they mean.

archaeologist - a person who learns about the past by digging things up.

ruins - old or abandoned buildings, or parts of buildings.

metal detector - a machine that beeps if it finds something metal.

trowel - a pointed tool archaeologists use for digging.

preserve - to protect something so it doesn't rot away.

remains - what's left of old bodies or ancient objects.

tomb - a place where an important person is buried.

Usborne Quicklinks

Would you like to find out more about digging up the past? You can visit Usborne Quicklinks for links to websites with videos, amazing facts and a quiz.

Go to **usborne.com/Quicklinks** and type in the keywords "**beginners digging**". Make sure you ask a grown-up before going online.

Notes for grown-ups

Please read the internet safety guidelines at Usborne Quicklinks with your child. Children should be supervised online. The websites are regularly reviewed and the links at Usborne Quicklinks are updated. However, Usborne Publishing is not responsible and does not accept liability for the content or availability of any website other than its own.

These clay statues were dug up in Nigeria. They were made around 2,000 years ago.

Index

archaeologist, 2, 6-7, 13, 20-21, 24, 26, 28, 30
battles, 20-21
bodies, 10, 13
bones, 7, 21
buildings, 5, 8-9, 12, 26-27
clothes, 10, 11
coins, 5, 24, 25
gold, 3, 14, 19
helmet, 29
huts, 9
jewels, 3, 14, 19
palace, 8, 26-27
plane, 20
pots, 16
preserving, 28-29, 30
pyramids, 23
mask, 15
metal detector, 5, 30
ornaments, 3, 14
ruins, 5, 8, 12, 30
shipwrecks, 16-17
statues, 18, 22, 29, 31
tombs, 18-19, 23, 30
town, 12
trowel, 6, 30

Acknowledgements

Photographic manipulation by Nick Wakeford and John Russell
Photo research by Ruth King

Photo credits

The publishers are grateful to the following for permission to reproduce material: **cover** © Ingo Jezierski/Photolibrary.com; **p1** © BAA, Oxford Archaeology and Wessex Archaeology; **p3** © The Trustees of the British Museum; **p4** © Adrian Warren/www.lastrefuge.co.uk; **p7** © Daniel Aguilar/Reuters/Corbis; **p8** © Stella Stella/Photolibrary.com; **p11** © Museum of London; **p12** © De Agostini/Getty Images; **p14** © Reuters/Eddie Keogh; **p15** © The Trustees of the British Museum; **p16** © Jonathan Blair/Corbis; **p18** © Morales Morales/Photolibrary.com; **p19** © Tony Kurdzuk/Star Ledger/Corbis; **p20** © Mirko Zanni/Photolibrary.com; **p22** © Superstock/Photolibrary.com; **p26-27** © Persepolis3d.com; **p29** © The Trustees of the British Museum; **p31** © akg-images/CDA/Guillemot.

Every effort has been made to trace and acknowledge ownership of copyright. If any rights have been omitted, the publishers offer to rectify this in any subsequent editions following notification.

This edition first published in 2021 by Usborne Publishing Ltd., Usborne House, 83-85 Saffron Hill, London EC1N 8RT, England. usborne.com Copyright © 2021, 2010 Usborne Publishing Ltd. All rights reserved. The name Usborne and the Balloon logo are Trade Marks of Usborne Publishing Ltd. No part of this publication may be reproduced, stored in a retrieval system, or transmitted in any form or by any means without the prior permission of Usborne Publishing Ltd. U.E.

EGYPTIANS

Stephanie Turnbull
Designed by Laura Parker
Illustrated by Colin King

Additional illustrations by Tim Haggerty
Egypt consultant: Miriam Bibby
Reading consultant: Alison Kelly

Contents

3 People of the past
4 River life
6 Farmers
8 At home
10 Kings of Egypt
12 Gods and goddesses
14 Temples
16 Making a mummy
18 Giant pyramids
20 Underground tombs
22 Hidden treasure
24 Fun and games
26 Dressing up
28 Egyptian writing
30 Glossary
31 Usborne Quicklinks
32 Index

People of the past

Egypt is a hot country in north Africa. The people who lived there thousands of years ago are called ancient Egyptians.

This picture is part of an ancient Egyptian wall painting. It shows a group of servants.

Egyptian paintings often show things from the side.

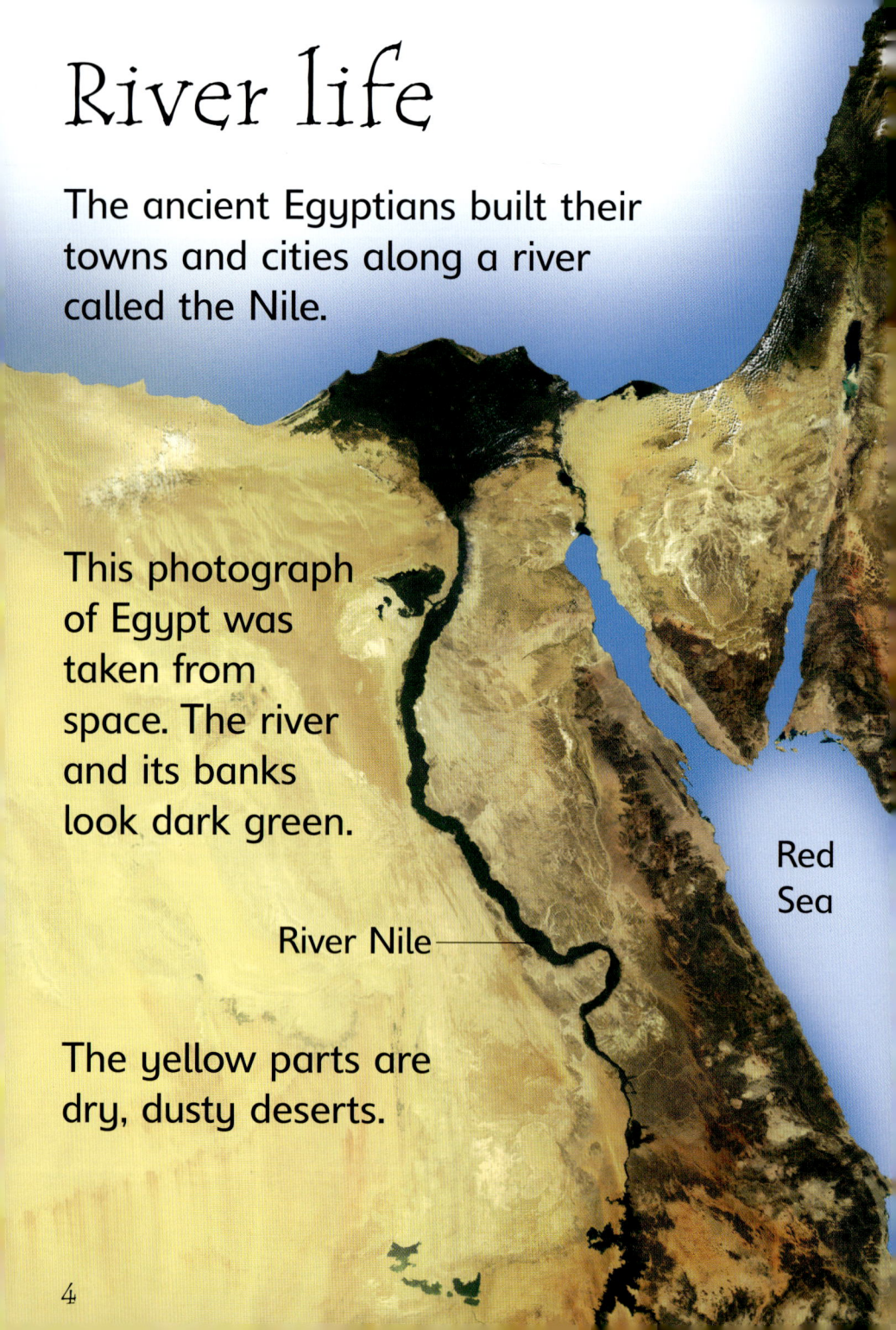

River life

The ancient Egyptians built their towns and cities along a river called the Nile.

This photograph of Egypt was taken from space. The river and its banks look dark green.

River Nile

Red Sea

The yellow parts are dry, dusty deserts.

The Egyptians fished in the river and sailed boats on it.

They drank water from it and used it for washing clothes.

This is an ancient Egyptian model of a boat.

People swam in the Nile, but they had to watch out for crocodiles.

Farmers

Egyptian farmers grew fruit, vegetables and other plants on the banks of the Nile.

This Egyptian painting shows farmers picking the grapes they have grown.

Farmers trained monkeys to pick fruit from high trees and throw it down.

The Nile flooded every year. This made the soil good for growing plants.

When the land dried up, plants grew in the sun. Farmers worked hard in the fields.

Farmers kept some of the crops to eat, and took the rest to markets.

At home

Ancient Egyptian houses were made of dried mud and painted white.

Houses had small windows to keep out the hot sun.

People cooked food and baked bread outside.

Some people had a pool in their garden where they kept fish to eat.

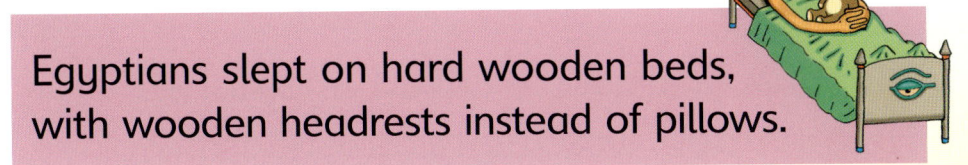

Egyptians slept on hard wooden beds, with wooden headrests instead of pillows.

Rich people often had servants. This model shows servants hard at work baking bread.

Kings of Egypt

Egyptian kings were called pharaohs. The pharaoh was the richest and most important person in the whole country.

A pharaoh made laws and gave orders.

He led his soldiers to fight enemies.

He went out hunting in his chariot.

He also met visitors from other countries.

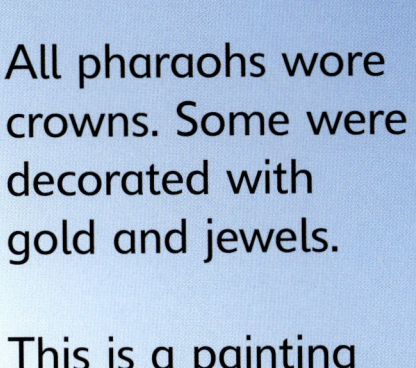

All pharaohs wore crowns. Some were decorated with gold and jewels.

This is a painting of Ramesses III. He is wearing a gold crown and a long, striped headdress.

Pharaoh Ramesses II had a pet lion to scare away enemies.

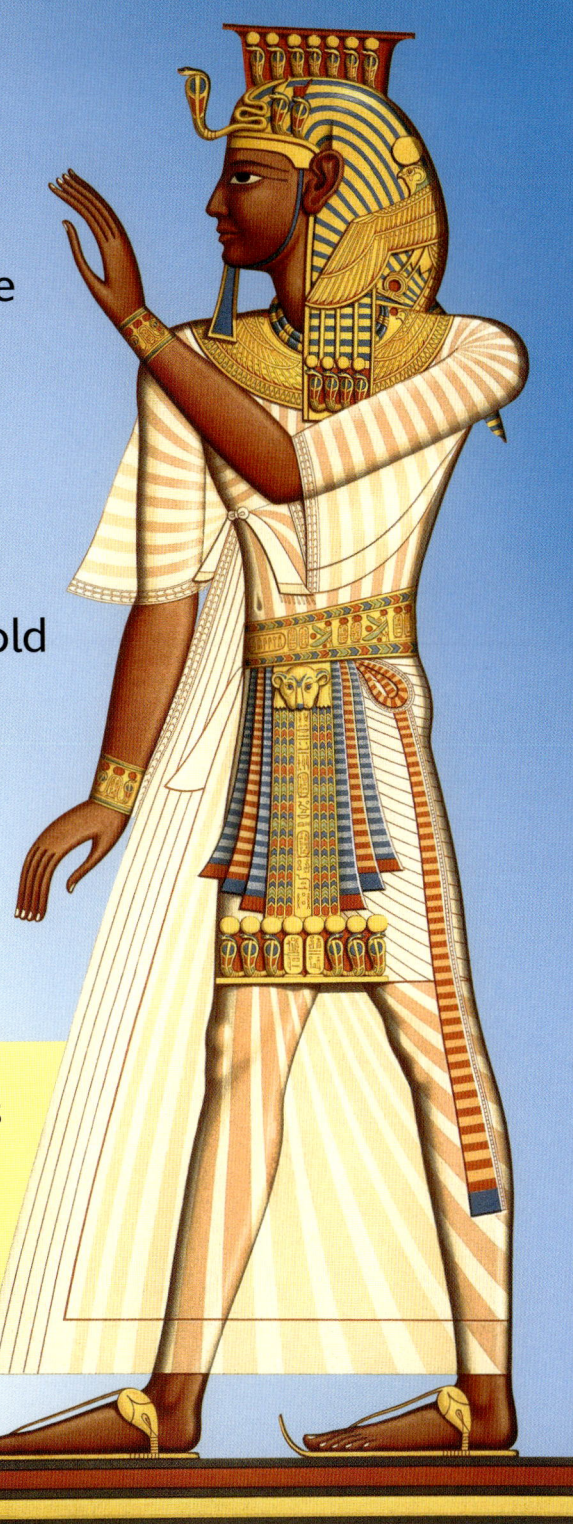

Gods and goddesses

Ancient Egyptians believed in many different gods and goddesses.

Egyptian gods sometimes looked like animals. This goddess, called Hathor, was often shown as a cow.

In this wall painting, Hathor has the horns of a cow on her crown.

Sekhmet was a fierce war goddess.

Ra was the powerful sun god.

Bes looked after children and families.

Ma'at was the goddess of truth.

Horus looked after pharaohs.

Seth was the evil uncle of Horus.

Horus and Seth were enemies. They once turned into fierce hippos to fight.

Temples

The Egyptians built huge stone temples to worship pharaohs and gods.

This is the temple of Pharaoh Ramesses II. Each statue outside the temple is more than ten times taller than a person.

In a temple, priests prayed to a statue of a god or pharaoh.

On special days, they carried the statue through the town.

This is a statue of Anubis, a god who could change into an animal called a jackal.

People often had small statues of gods at home, too.

Making a mummy

When an important person died, Egyptians wrapped their body so it didn't rot. This is called making a mummy.

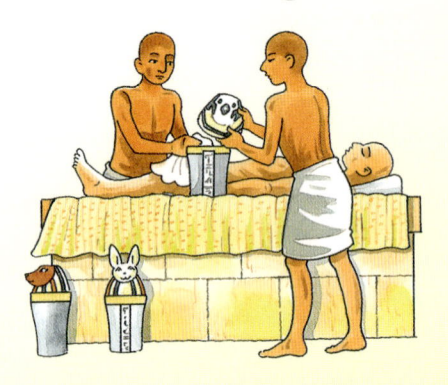

1. First they took out the person's insides and put them in pots.

2. Then they packed the body in salt to dry it out.

3. Next, they wrapped the body tightly in bandages.

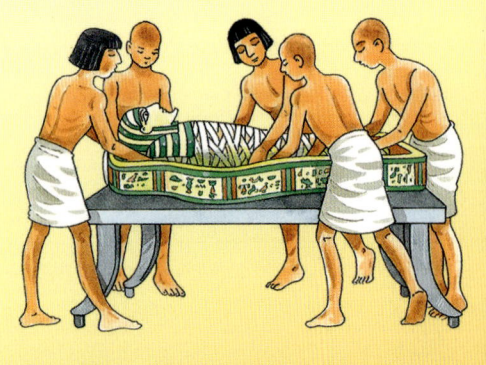

4. Finally, they put a mask on the mummy and laid it in a coffin.

Egyptians made animal mummies too.

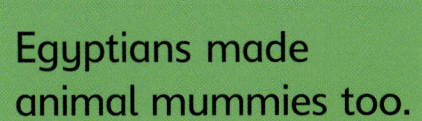

The person's insides were kept in pots with lids like these. Each pot has a god's head.

Coffins were shaped to look like a person and covered with spells and pictures.

Giant pyramids

When a pharaoh died, his coffin was put inside an enormous stone pyramid.

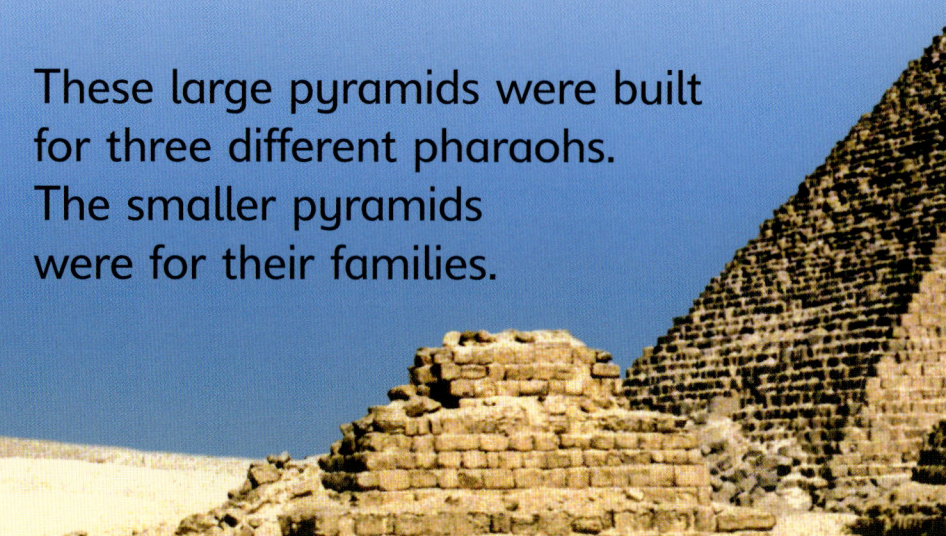

These large pyramids were built for three different pharaohs. The smaller pyramids were for their families.

Workers cut stone blocks and dragged them along.

They pulled the blocks up a ramp, onto the pyramid.

After many years of work, they put the last stone on top.

Finally, workers made the pyramid smooth and shiny.

19

Underground tombs

After many years, Egyptians stopped building pyramids. They buried important people in underground tombs instead.

1. First, workers dug a deep tunnel into a rocky cliff.

2. Then they built rooms and corridors underground.

3. They painted the walls and filled the rooms with treasure.

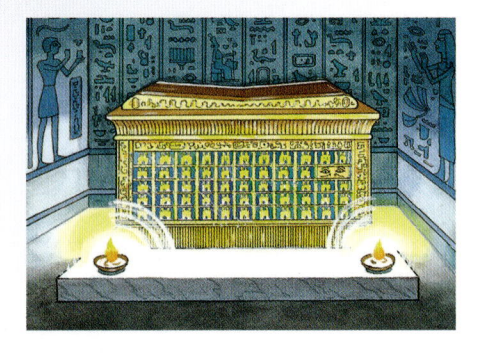

4. They put the coffin inside a huge box in a special room.

This is the tomb of a man named Peshedu.
His coffin lay in the room through this arch.

Robbers often dug into tombs and pyramids to steal treasure.

Hidden treasure

The tomb of the pharaoh Tutankhamun was hidden for thousands of years.

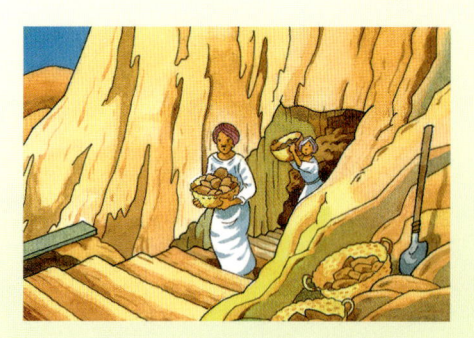

In 1922, explorers found a secret door, hidden behind rocks.

Inside were rooms crammed with glittering treasure.

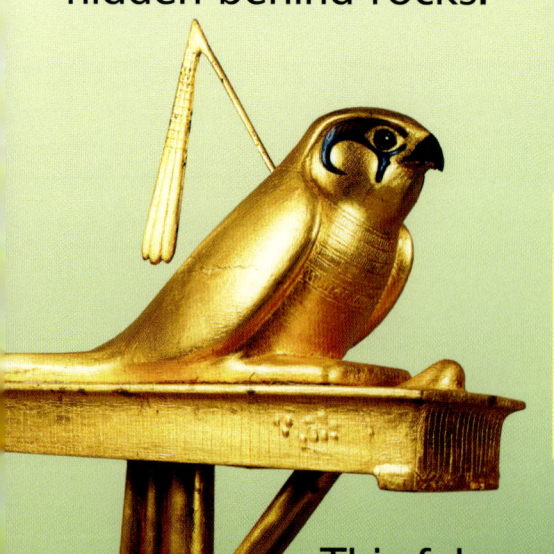

It took ten years to clear the tomb and list all the amazing treasures.

This falcon was one of the many beautiful statues in the tomb.

This big, heavy mask covered the face of Tutankhamun's mummy.

It is made of gold and thin strips of glass.

Fun and games

Egyptians loved sports and games, as well as music, dancing and parties.

Some people learned to play instruments, like this harp.

Men liked to have boating contests on the River Nile.

The team that pushed the other boat over won the game.

This painting shows a man hunting with his family. He is standing on a boat and throwing a stick at birds.

At parties, people enjoyed watching dancers perform all kinds of difficult moves.

Dressing up

Egyptians liked to look good. They wore simple, flowing clothes and lots of jewels.

This wide, gold necklace is shaped like a bird. It was made for a pharaoh.

People often put perfumed fat on their heads. As it melted, it made them smell nice.

Men and women wore loose, light skirts and dresses that kept them cool.

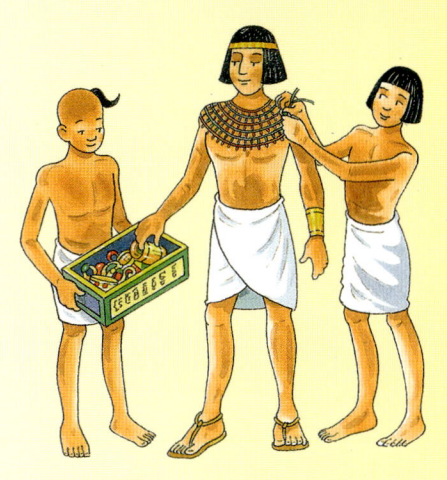

They decorated the clothes with rings, bracelets, necklaces and other jewels.

Everyone wore make-up too. They put lots of dark paint around their eyes.

Most people shaved their heads to keep cool. Adults usually wore wigs.

Egyptian writing

Egyptian writing was made up of lots of pictures called hieroglyphs.

People called scribes could read and write hieroglyphs. The statue below shows a scribe.

A scribe's job was to write letters and keep records.

He also had to teach children to read and write.

These hieroglyphs were painted on a tomb.
They are spells to protect a dead person.

Most ordinary people didn't have a clue what hieroglyphs meant.

Glossary

Here are some of the words in this book you might not know. This page tells you what they mean.

pharaoh - the title ancient Egyptians gave their king.

temple - a place where Egyptians went to worship gods and dead pharaohs.

priest - a person who worked in a temple. Priests prayed to statues.

mummy - a body that has been dried out to make it last for many years.

tomb - a place under the ground where a person was buried.

scribe - a person whose job was to read and write.

hieroglyph - a picture or symbol. Egyptians wrote using hieroglyphs.

Usborne Quicklinks

Would you like to find out more about the the Egyptians? You can visit Usborne Quicklinks for links to websites with videos, amazing facts and things to make and do.

Go to **usborne.com/Quicklinks** and type in the keywords **"beginners Egyptians"**. Make sure you ask a grown-up before going online.

Notes for grown-ups

Please read the internet safety guidelines at Usborne Quicklinks with your child. Children should be supervised online. The websites are regularly reviewed and the links at Usborne Quicklinks are updated. However, Usborne Publishing is not responsible and does not accept liability for the content or availability of any website other than its own.

This photo shows the Great Sphinx of Giza, built by the ancient Egyptians. It has the body of a lion and the head of a man.

Index

boats, 5, 24, 25
clothes, 26–27
coffins, 16, 17, 20, 21
dancing, 24, 25
Egypt, 3, 4
farming, 6–7
fishing, 5
food, 6, 7, 8, 9
gods and goddesses,
    12–13, 14, 15, 17
hieroglyphs, 28–29, 30
homes, 8–9
hunting, 10, 25
jewels, 11, 26, 27
markets, 7
masks, 16, 23

mummies, 16–17, 23, 30
musical instruments, 24
paintings, 3, 6, 11, 12, 20,
    25, 29
parties, 24, 25
pharaohs, 10–11, 14, 15,
    18, 22–23, 26, 30
priests, 15, 30
pyramids, 18–19, 21
River Nile, 4–5, 6, 7
scribes, 28, 30
sports, 24, 25
statues, 14, 15, 22, 28
temples, 14–15, 30
tombs, 20–21, 22, 29, 30
Tutankhamun, 22–23

Acknowledgements

Photographic manipulation by Emma Julings

Photo credits

The publishers are grateful to the following for permission to reproduce material:
cover © Kenneth Garrett; **p1** © Sandro Vannini/Corbis; **p2-3** © Gianni Dagli Orti/Corbis; **p4** © NASA (Jacques Descloitres, MODIS Land Science Team); **p5** © The Trustees of the British Museum; **p6** © Gianni Dagli Orti/Corbis; **p9** © Gianni Dagli Orti/Corbis; **p11** © Heritage Images (The British Library)/Topfoto; **p12** © Ancient Art & Architecture Collection Ltd/Alamy; **p14** © Richard Passmore/Getty Images; **p15** © Sandro Vannini/Corbis; **p17 top** © The Trustees of the British Museum; **p17 bottom** © Dagli Orti/ Musée du Louvre Paris/The Art Archive; **p18-19** © Brian Lawrence/Alamy; **p21** © Gianni Dagli Orti/Corbis; **p22** © Sandro Vannini/Corbis; **p23** © Alvis Upitis/Getty Images; **p24** © The Trustees of the British Museum; **p25** © The Gallery Collection/Corbis; **p26** © Bettman/Corbis; **p28** © Roger Wood/Corbis; **p29** © Wolfgang Kaehler/Corbis; **p31** © Brian Lawrence/Alamy.

Every effort has been made to trace and acknowledge ownership of copyright. If any rights have been omitted, the publishers offer to rectify this in any subsequent editions following notification.

This edition first published in 2020 by Usborne Publishing Ltd., 83-85 Saffron Hill, London EC1N 8RT, England. usborne.com Copyright © 2020, 2015, 2006, 2004 Usborne Publishing Ltd. All rights reserved. The name Usborne and the Balloon logo are Trade Marks of Usborne Publishing Ltd. No part of this publication may be reproduced, stored in a retrieval system, or transmitted in any form or by any means without the prior permission of Usborne Publishing Ltd. U.E.

Ancient Greeks

Stephanie Turnbull

Designed by Catherine-Anne MacKinnon
and Vici Leyhane

Illustrated by Colin King

Additional design by Helen Wood and Laura Parker
Additional illustrations by Uwe Mayer
Greek consultant: Dr. Katharine Haynes
Reading consultant: Alison Kelly

Contents

- 3 An ancient land
- 4 Life in Greece
- 6 Clothes and fashion
- 8 What people ate
- 10 A trip to market
- 12 Feasts and fun
- 14 Gods and goddesses
- 16 Talking to the gods
- 18 Heroes and monsters
- 20 The Olympic Games
- 22 Greek plays
- 24 Mighty warriors
- 26 Into battle
- 28 Great Greeks
- 30 Glossary
- 31 Usborne Quicklinks
- 32 Index

An ancient land

Greece is a hot country in southern Europe. The ancient Greeks lived there about three thousand years ago.

Many Greek towns were near the sea. Boats carried people from place to place.

Life in Greece

Some Greeks lived in busy towns or cities. Others lived far out in the countryside.

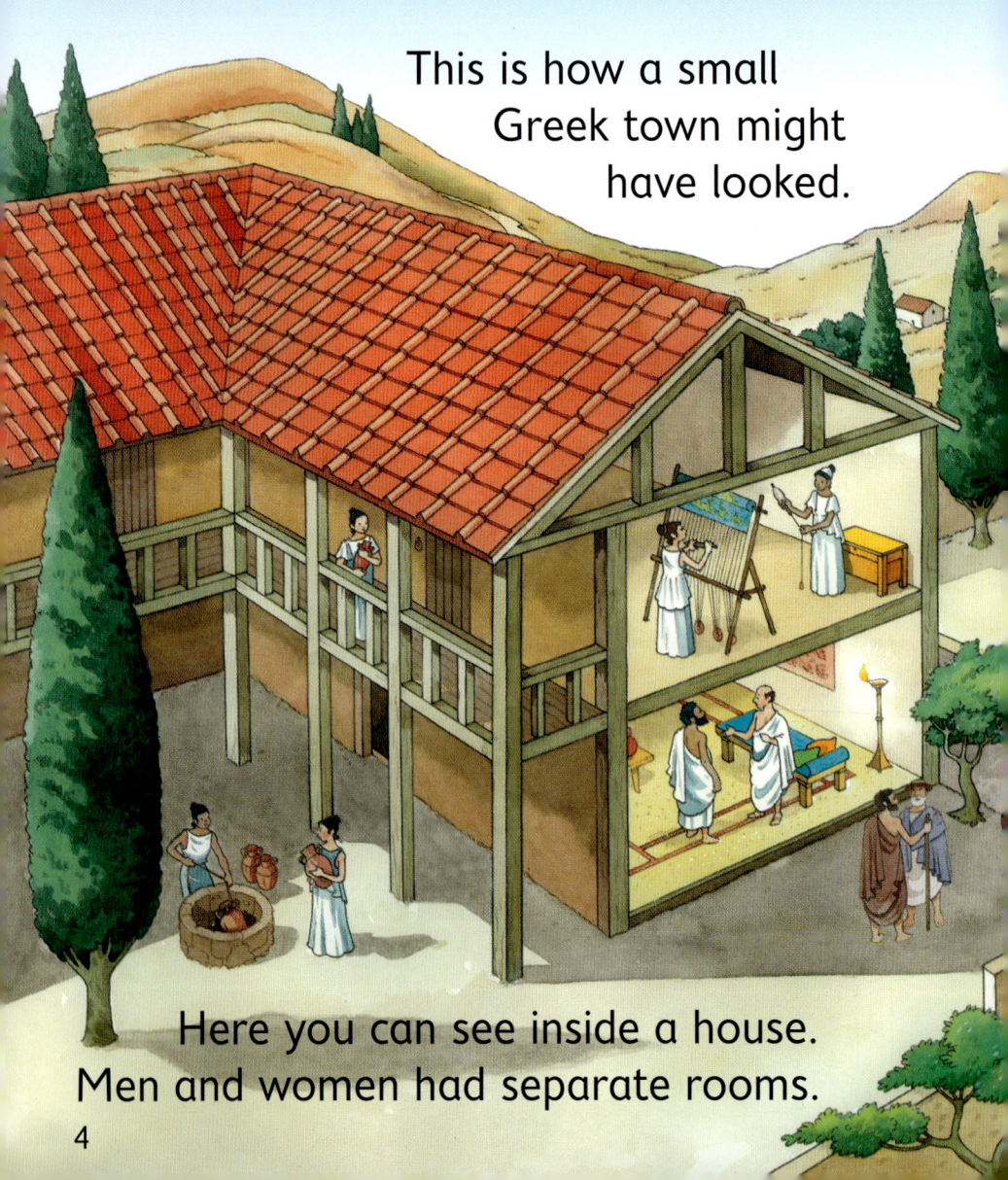

This is how a small Greek town might have looked.

Here you can see inside a house. Men and women had separate rooms.

Temples and other important buildings stood on hills.

Greek houses were made of wood and mud bricks.

Rich people had slaves to do the housework for them.

Clothes and fashion

The Greeks liked to wear simple, loose clothes that kept them cool.

Women always wore long tunics called chitons.

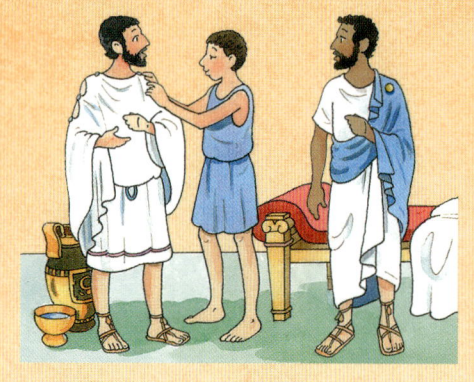

Men wore long or short tunics, often with a cloak.

Rich women had earrings like these, made from gold.

This ancient Greek statue shows a woman dressed in outdoor clothes.

She is wearing a sunhat and a cloak to protect her from the Sun.

Many Greek men had beards. It was fashionable to keep them neatly trimmed.

What people ate

Most Greek people ate lots of vegetables, fruit and other fresh foods.

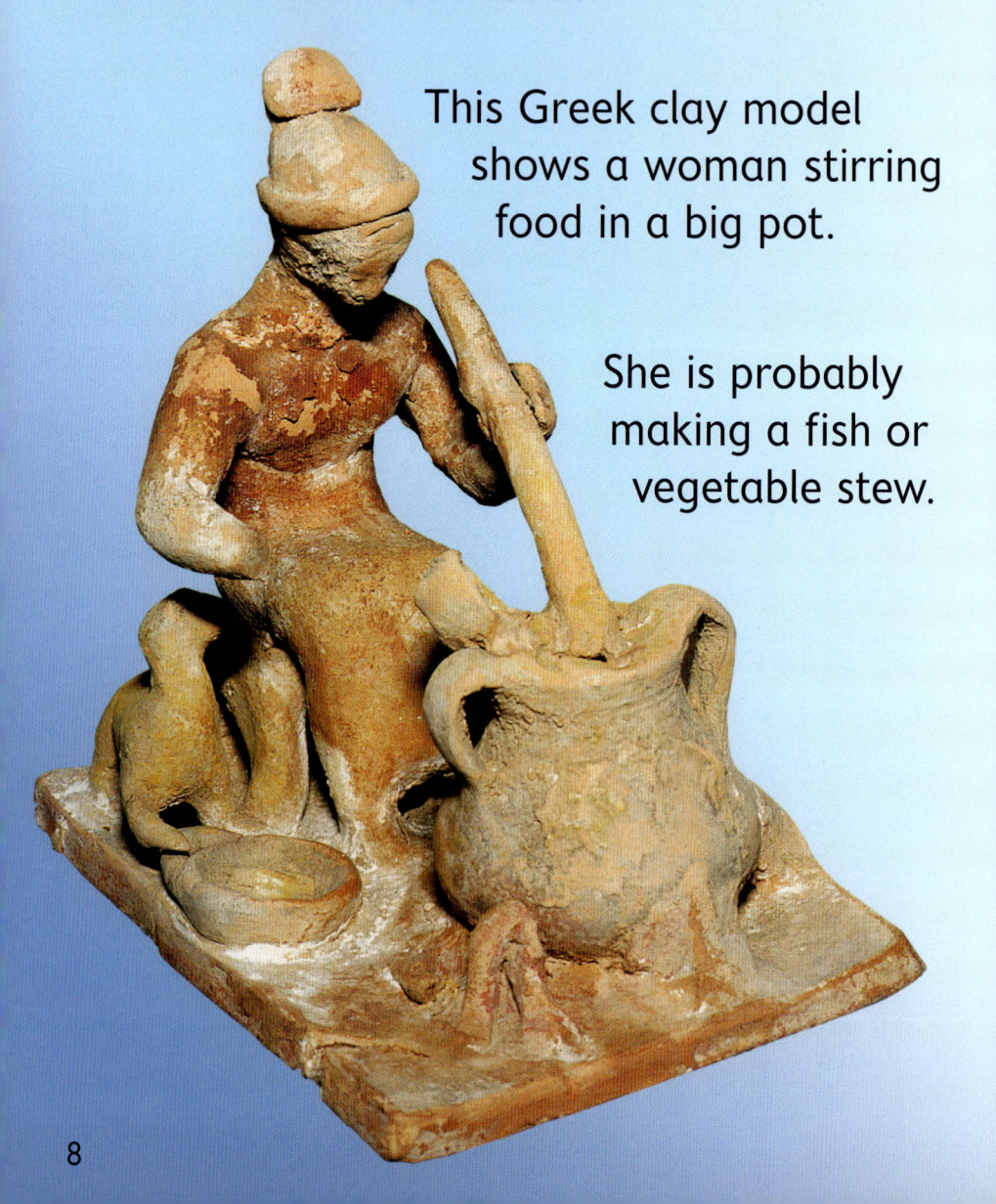

This Greek clay model shows a woman stirring food in a big pot.

She is probably making a fish or vegetable stew.

Farmers grew crops that were used for making bread.

Often people kept a few goats and sheep for their milk.

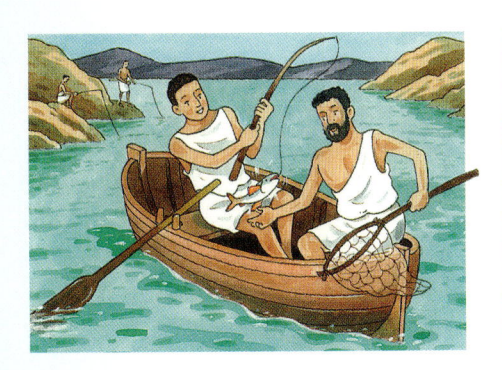

People who lived near the sea caught fresh fish to eat.

There were plenty of olives to knock down from olive trees.

Poor people just ate lumpy porridge made from flour and water.

A trip to market

The market was the busiest part of every ancient Greek town.

At the market there were lots of stalls selling fresh food.

People stood and chatted with friends or had meetings.

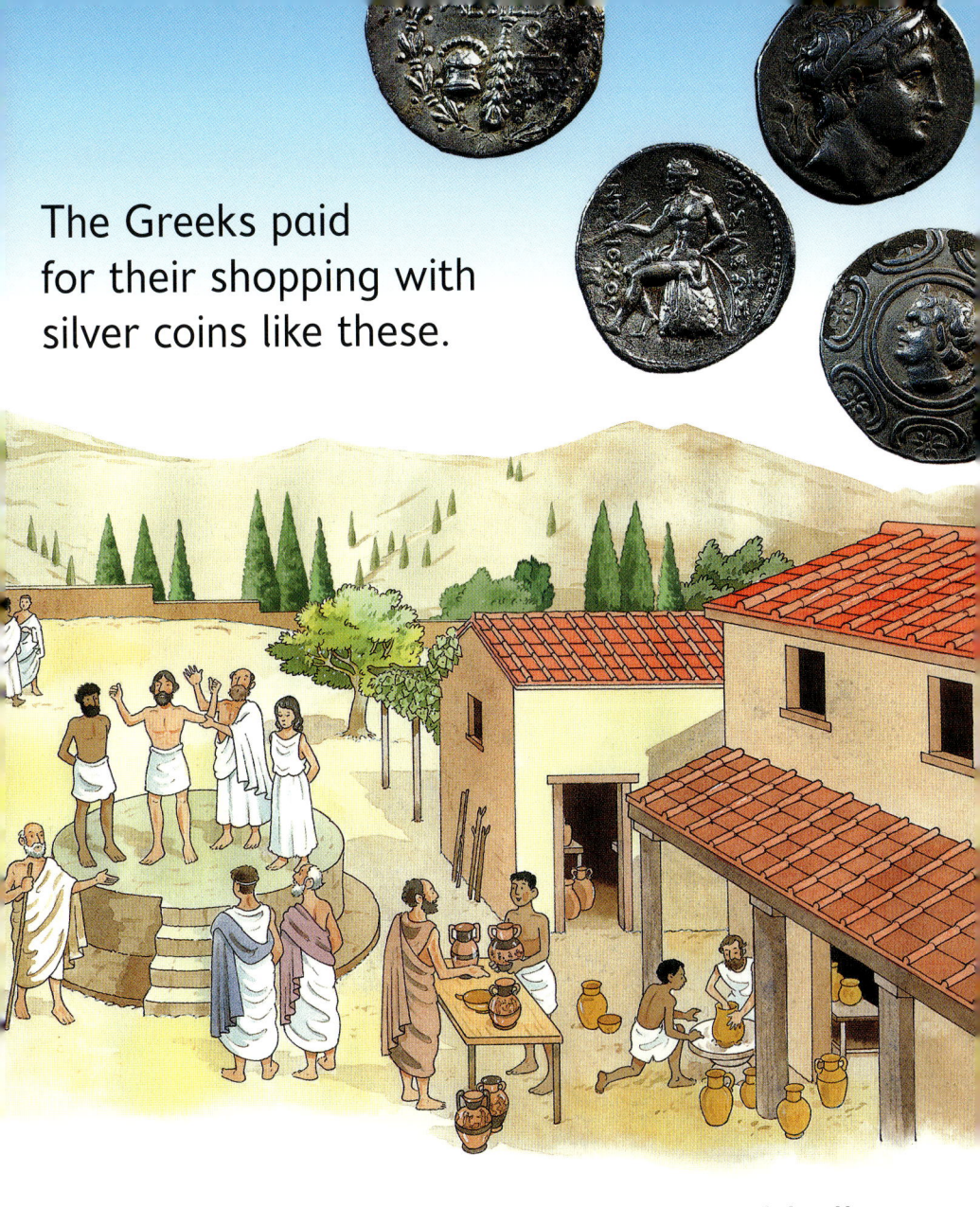

The Greeks paid for their shopping with silver coins like these.

Slaves stood on a round platform, waiting to be sold.

Craftsmen sold all kinds of pots from their workshops.

11

Feasts and fun

The Greeks loved to have big feasts. Usually these parties were just for men.

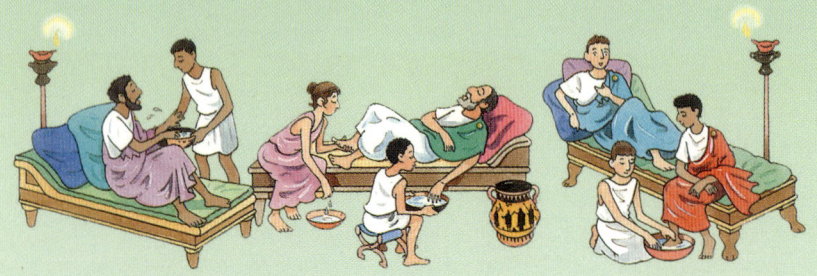

As visitors arrived, slaves washed their hands and feet.

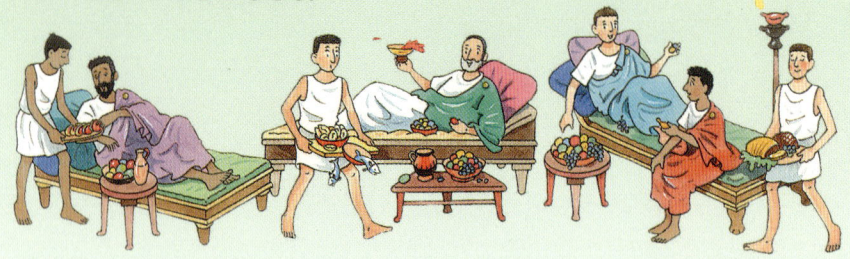

Everyone ate plenty of meat, fish, cheese and vegetables, then fruit and cakes.

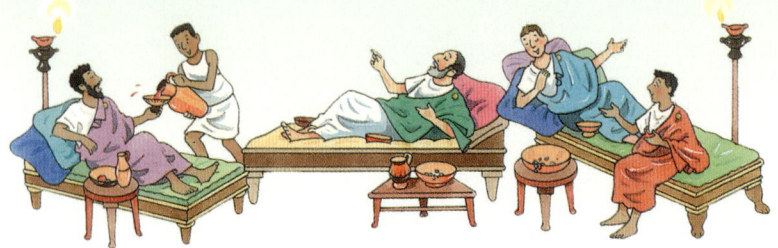

The guests stayed for hours, drinking wine and talking.

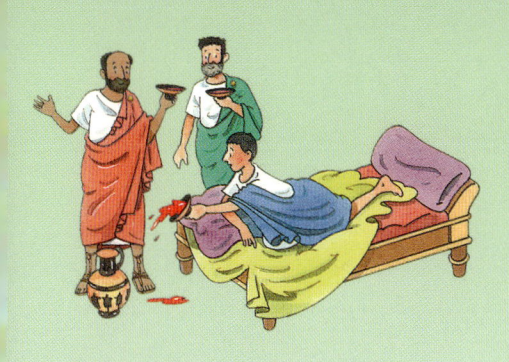

Men played a game where they threw wine at a target.

If they missed, they had to have another drink and try again.

Some feasts had music too. This painting of a Greek party shows a musician playing two flutes.

Gods and goddesses

The Greeks believed in many gods and goddesses, and told hundreds of stories about them.

This is a statue of Artemis, the Greek goddess of hunting.

She lived in the forest and hunted animals with arrows.

Zeus was the king of the gods. He was married to Hera, a beautiful goddess.

Zeus' brother, Poseidon, ruled the sea. He lived in an underwater palace.

Athene was Zeus' daughter. She was the strict, wise goddess of war.

Hades was king of the Underworld, where all dead people were taken.

If Zeus was angry with someone, he hurled lightning down at them.

Talking to the gods

Gods and goddesses were very important to the Greeks.

In temples, people prayed to statues of gods for help.

They also brought presents to make the gods happy.

There were festivals for gods, with music, dancing and sports.

Priestesses gave people messages from the gods.

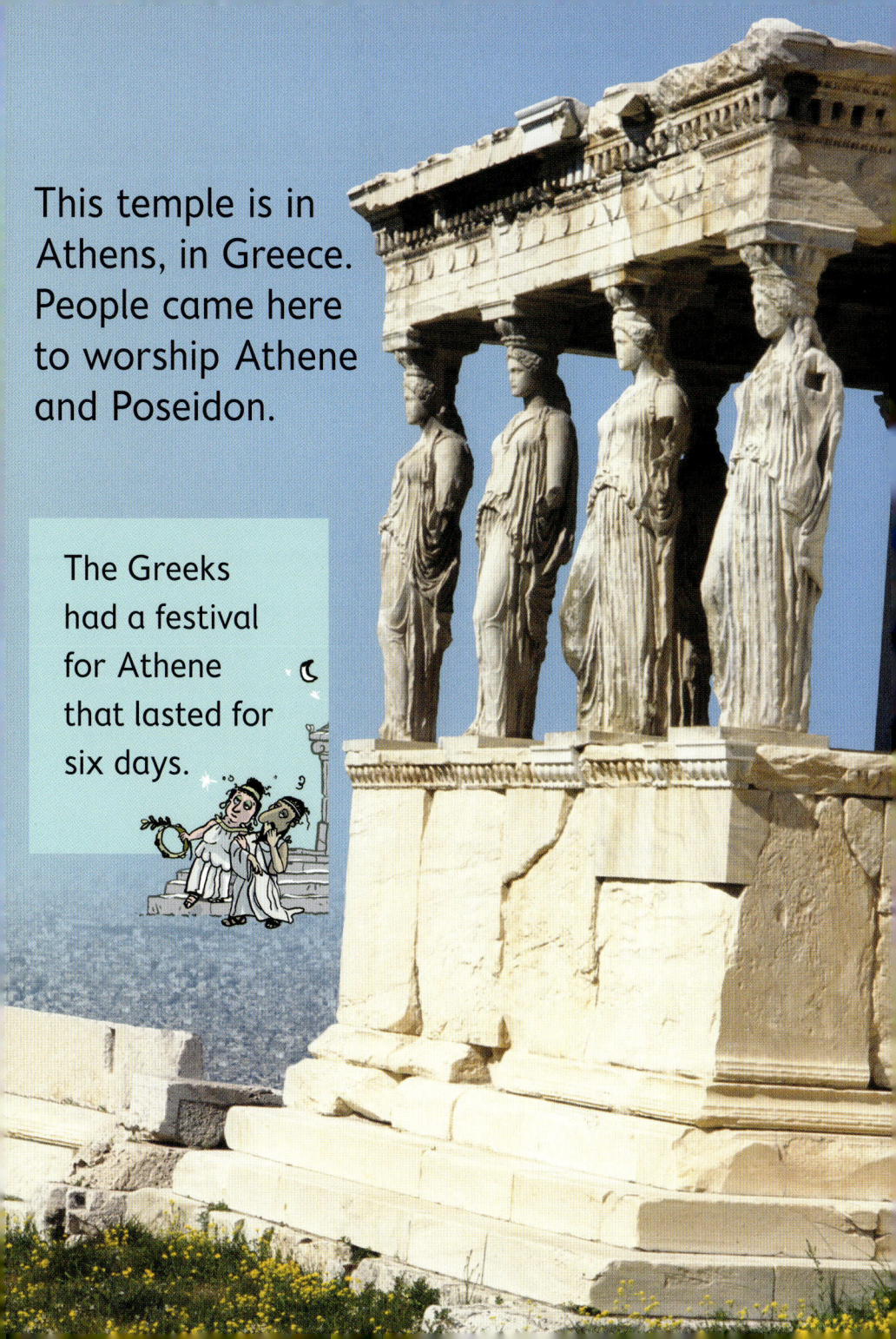

This temple is in Athens, in Greece. People came here to worship Athene and Poseidon.

The Greeks had a festival for Athene that lasted for six days.

Heroes and monsters

There are many myths about brave Greek heroes and the terrible beasts they fought.

The monster Medusa turned men to stone if they looked at her.

A clever young man named Perseus set out to kill Medusa.

He used his shield as a mirror, so he never looked at her.

Perseus cut off the monster's head and came home a hero.

This painting from a pot shows a hero called Heracles, killing a terrifying monster.

Heracles was half-man and half-god, which made him very strong.

The Olympic Games

The Olympic Games began in Olympia, in ancient Greece. They were made up of many sports. They still exist today.

These runners are taking part in the modern Olympics.

At the ancient Olympics there were wrestling matches.

Some athletes hurled a discus as far as they could.

The modern Olympics are held all over the world. Only the best athletes take part.

Another popular Olympic sport was the long jump.

Men raced around a track in chariots pulled by horses.

Greek plays

Many Greeks enjoyed going to see plays, which were shown outside.

People sat in rows on stone seats.

The actors had lots of space to perform.

People watched plays here in ancient times. You can still see seats and part of the stage.

Greek actors wore masks to show what their characters were like. This mask shows a funny old man.

Some plays were tragedies. These had a sad ending.

Other plays were comedies, which made people laugh.

Only men were allowed to act in plays.

Mighty warriors

Some Greek men trained to be soldiers. A few soldiers rode on horses, but many others marched on foot.

This picture from a Greek pot shows foot soldiers fighting with long, pointed spears.

A Greek soldier wore metal plates to protect his body.

Metal plates called greaves were strapped to his legs.

A large helmet covered his head and neck.

He carried a sharp spear and a flat metal shield.

Soldiers had swords too. This is a modern copy of a Greek sword and its holder.

25

Into battle

The Greeks had wars with other countries, and sometimes with each other too.

Most of the fighting was done on foot. Groups of soldiers charged at each other.

Soldiers often attacked enemy cities. They broke down the walls and stormed in.

There were many sea battles. Ships called triremes tried to ram each other.

This modern ship has been built to look just like an ancient Greek trireme.

People sit inside the ship and row with long oars.

One part of Greece, called Sparta, was famous for its strong, fearless fighters.

Great Greeks

Many clever people lived in ancient Greece.

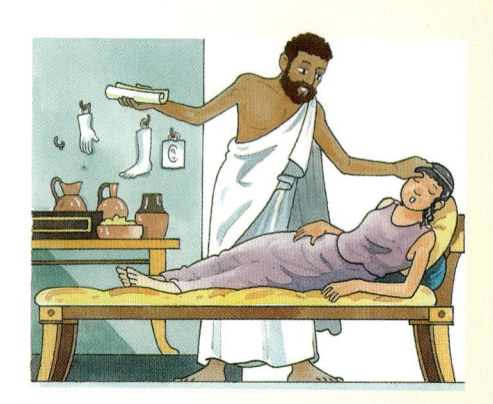

Hippocrates was a doctor who learned how bodies worked.

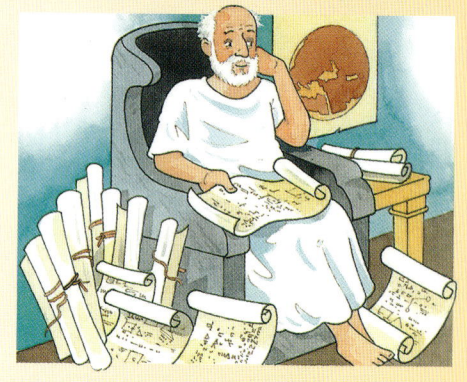

Aristotle studied science and wrote many books.

Sappho was a rich woman who wrote beautiful poems.

Pericles was a wise leader who ruled the city of Athens.

Alexander the
Great was a brave soldier.
This picture shows him riding into battle.

Alexander always wanted to be a hero.

When he grew up, he ruled all of Greece.

Some Greeks were inventors, but many of their machines didn't work.

Glossary

Here are some of the words in this book you might not know. This page tells you what they mean.

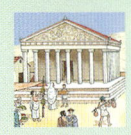

temple - a place where the ancient Greeks prayed to statues of gods.

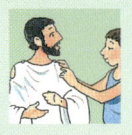

chiton - a long or short dress made from one piece of material.

priestess - a woman who worked in a temple and spoke to the gods.

shield - a flat metal plate. Soldiers used shields to protect themselves.

discus - a round metal or stone plate used in throwing competitions.

chariot - a small cart with two wheels that was pulled by horses.

trireme - a powerful Greek warship with three rows of oars on each side.

Usborne Quicklinks

Would you like to find out more about the ancient Greeks? You can visit Usborne Quicklinks for links to websites with videos, amazing facts and things to make and do.

Go to **usborne.com/Quicklinks** and type in the keywords **"beginners ancient Greeks"**.
Make sure you ask a grown-up before going online.

Notes for grown-ups

Please read the internet safety guidelines at Usborne Quicklinks with your child. Children should be supervised online. The websites are regularly reviewed and the links at Usborne Quicklinks are updated. However, Usborne Publishing is not responsible and does not accept liability for the content or availability of any website other than its own.

This Greek jug is 2,600 years old. It has an animal's head for its spout.

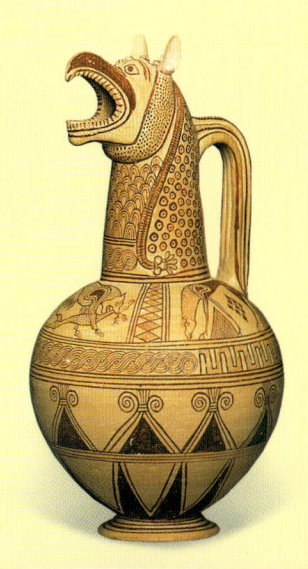

Index

Alexander the Great, 29
Aristotle, 28
Athens, 17, 28
battles, 24, 26-27
boats, 3, 26, 27
clothes, 6-7
farming, 9
feasts, 12-13
festivals, 16, 17
food, 8-9, 10, 12
gods and goddesses, 14-15, 16-17, 19
Heracles, 19
Hippocrates, 28
houses, 4-5
markets, 10-11
masks, 23
Medusa, 18
money, 11
music, 13, 16
Olympic Games, 20-21
Pericles, 28
Perseus, 18
plays, 22-23
priestesses, 16, 30
Sappho, 28
shields, 18, 25, 30
slaves, 5, 11, 12
soldiers, 24-25, 26, 27, 29
spears, 24, 25
sports, 16, 20-21
swords, 25
temples, 5, 16, 17, 30
towns, 3, 4-5, 10-11

Acknowledgements
Photographic manipulation by Mike Wheatley

Photo credits

The publishers are grateful to the following for permission to reproduce material. **Cover** © Procession of horsemen, 445-438 BC, by Phidias, Detail/British Museum, London, UK/ De Agostini Picture Library/Bridgeman Images; **p1** © The Art Archive/Kanellopoulos Museum Athens/Dagli Orti; **p6** © The Trustees of the British Museum; **p7** © The Trustees of the British Museum; **p8** © CM Dixon/Heritage Images; **p11** © The Art Archive/Kanellopoulos Museum Athens/Dagli Orti; **p13** © The Art Archive/Bibliothèque des Arts Décoratifs Paris/ Dagli Orti; **p14** © The Bridgeman Art Library/The Louvre/Peter Willi; **p17** © Alamy/Webphotographer/Nebojsa Basic; **p19** © The Trustees of the British Museum; **p20-21** © Corbis/Le Segretain Pascal/Corbis Sygma; **p22** © Corbis/Roger Wood; **p23** © The Art Archive/ Archaeological Museum Piraeus/Dagli Orti; **p24** © The Art Archive/National Archaeological Museum Athens/Dagli Orti; **p25** © Ancient-Empires.com; **p27** © Ancient Art and Architecture Collection/Mike Andrews; **p29** © Corbis/Mimmo Jodice; **p31** © The Trustees of the British Museum

Every effort has been made to trace and acknowledge ownership of copyright. If any rights have been omitted, the publishers offer to rectify this in any subsequent editions following notification.

This edition first published in 2020 by Usborne Publishing Ltd., Usborne House, 83-85 Saffron Hill, London EC1N 8RT, England usborne.com Copyright © 2020, 2015, 2007, 2004 Usborne Publishing Ltd. All rights reserved. The name Usborne and the Balloon logo are Trade Marks of Usborne Publishing Ltd. No part of this publication may be reproduced, stored in a retrieval system, or transmitted in any form or by any means without the prior permission of Usborne Publishing Ltd. U.E.

The Celts

Leonie Pratt

Designed by Zöe Wray

Illustrated by Terry McKenna

Consultant: Dr. James E. Fraser, University of Edinburgh

Reading consultant: Alison Kelly, Roehampton University

Contents

- 3   Iron Age Celts
- 4   Meet the tribe
- 6   High on a hill
- 8   Village people
- 10   Farming and food
- 12   Looking good
- 14   Crafty Celts
- 16   Gifts for the gods
- 18   Festival fun
- 20   Fearsome fighters
- 22   Telling tales
- 24   Trouble ahead
- 26   Battling Britain
- 28   Celtic clues
- 30   Glossary
- 31   Usborne Quicklinks
- 32   Index

Iron Age Celts

The Celts were people who lived in Europe over 2,000 years ago. They lived during a time called the Iron Age.

In the Iron Age, people first started using a metal called iron to make tools for farming, and weapons such as swords and spears.

Meet the tribe

The Celts lived in groups called tribes.

The tribe leader was a chief, a king, or sometimes a queen.

The best fighters in the tribe became fierce warriors.

Bards told stories and poems about famous warriors.

Druids were priests. Everyone thought they were very wise.

Most people worked on the land, growing crops and taking care of animals.

Everyone shared everything with the other members of their tribe.

High on a hill

Different tribes didn't always get along. They often tried to steal things from each other, so many tribes built forts on hills to stay safe.

These are the ruins of a Celtic hillfort in Danebury in the south of England.

Tribes could see people coming from a long way away, because they were so high up.

Steep banks were cut into the hillside to make it hard for anyone to attack quickly.

There were only one or two entrances. This made the fort easy to defend.

Village people

People lived in round houses inside the hillfort.

The walls of the house were made from sticks.

The sticks were covered with mud to keep out wind and rain.

Grain was stored in pits in the ground.

Part of the house below has been cut away so you can see inside.

A fire kept the room warm.

Smoke escaped through the straw roof.

Everyone slept around the edge of one big room.

Farming and food

The Celts grew oats, wheat and barley. They used them to make porridge and bread.

1. Men cut the wheat using iron tools called sickles.

2. Women ground the grain into flour between two stones.

3. They mixed some water into the flour to make dough.

4. Then, they cooked the dough on a stone next to a fire.

The Celts had knives, but no forks - so they ate with their fingers.

Most meals were meat stews, vegetable stews, or porridge. The food was served from pots, jugs and pans like these ones.

Looking good

The Celts wanted their clothes to look good, as well as keep them warm.

Women used plants to dye wool, then wove it into patterned cloth.

Men wore tunics with baggy leggings and a belt. Women wore long dresses.

For extra warmth, people wore cloaks that were held in place with a brooch.

Celts liked wearing bracelets, and collars called torcs around their necks.

Only an important person would wear a gold torc like this one.

The ends of this torc can stretch apart to fit around a person's neck.

Very rich men brushed gold dust over their cloaks.

13

Crafty Celts

Celts were very good at making things from metal.

Bronze is a mixture of two metals, tin and copper. The Celts used it to make ornaments like this cow.

At first bronze is dark brown and shiny, but it turns green as it gets older.

1. A craftsman made a wax shape, then covered it in clay.

2. Then, he baked it to melt the wax and make the clay hard.

3. He poured out the wax, then poured in melted bronze.

4. The bronze set as it cooled then the clay was chipped off.

Gifts for the gods

The Celts believed in lots of different gods and goddesses. They tried to keep the gods happy by giving them gifts.

Druids collected gifts like weapons, tools and bronze brooches.

They put the gifts in a river or lake for the gods to find.

Druids sometimes killed people to give as gifts to the gods.

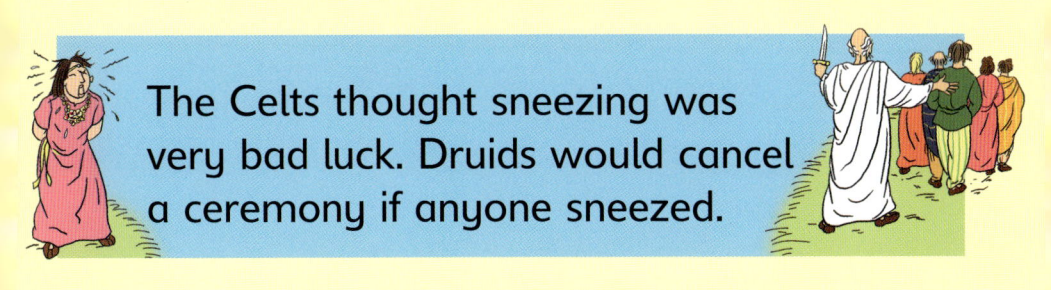

The Celts thought sneezing was very bad luck. Druids would cancel a ceremony if anyone sneezed.

This is the body of a Celt who was found in a bog in Denmark. Many people think he was killed by druids.

The mud has stopped his body from rotting away.

Festival fun

The Celts held festivals at different times of year to celebrate their gods and the seasons.

The Celts celebrated the end of winter with fires and feasts.

Men raced each other on horseback at the summer festival.

At one festival, the Celts thought that the world of the dead and the world of the living mixed together.

At the spring festival, cows and sheep were led between two bonfires.

The Celts thought this would stop them from getting sick.

Fearsome fighters

Celts were famous for being fierce, brave warriors. Different tribes sometimes fought to get each other's land.

Warriors spiked their hair to look scary.

They use a blue dye called woad to paint curly patterns on their bodies.

They blew trumpets called carnyxes to make a frightening noise.

Rich warriors rode on chariots and threw spears.

Some warriors fought using iron swords.

In a very big battle, women fought, too.

Some warriors went into battle wearing no clothes at all!

21

Telling tales

Warriors often had a feast after winning a battle. After the feast, the men boasted to each other about how brave they were.

The bard did the chief's boasting for him...

...and made fun of the chief's enemies.

If the chief liked what he heard, then he rewarded the bard with gold.

A good bard could become very, very rich.

22

Bards also told stories and poems about famous warriors. This is an old painting of a famous Celtic warrior called Cu Chulainn.

Trouble ahead

The Celts weren't the only people living in Europe. There were Greeks and Romans too.

The Romans were jealous when they saw that the Celts had such good farmland.

Julius Caesar led a large Roman army to attack the Celtic tribes in Gaul (now France).

Some of the tribes got together to fight back, but the Romans won in the end.

This is a statue of the leader of the Celtic tribes, Vercingetorix. He was killed by the Romans.

Battling Britain

The Romans also invaded Britain. Some tribes didn't like this and fought back.

Queen Boudica and thousands of Celts attacked some Roman towns, but the Romans fought them and lots of Celts were killed.

The Celts in England couldn't stop the Romans from taking over. But the Romans weren't able to take control of Scotland.

The Romans wanted to watch over the Celts in Scotland. They built this long wall, called Hadrian's wall, for soldiers to guard.

It took thousands of Romans about six years to build the wall.

Celtic clues

The Celts never wrote anything about themselves. People who study them have to use other clues to find out about them.

The Romans were interested in how the Celts lived and wrote lots about them.

People have found Celtic objects left in rivers and lakes as gifts for the gods.

Sometimes Celts were buried with chariots, weapons and other things.

This Celtic bowl has pictures around it showing people hunting and fighting. The big heads on the outside are gods.

Glossary

Here are some of the words in this book you might not know. This page tells you what they mean.

bard - a man who made up stories and poems and sang songs.

druid - a Celtic priest. Druids were very wise and important.

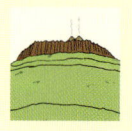

hillfort - a village with a wooden fence around it, built on top of a hill.

torc - a gold, silver or bronze collar that Celts wore around their necks.

woad - blue dye. Celts used woad to paint their bodies and dye clothes.

carnyx - a tall war trumpet. Warriors blew carnyxes to scare their enemies.

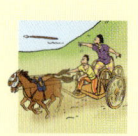

chariot – a cart pulled by two horses. Rich warriors rode chariots into battle.

Usborne Quicklinks

Would you like to find out more about the Celts? You can visit Usborne Quicklinks for links to websites with videos, amazing facts and things to make and do.

Go to **usborne.com/Quicklinks** and type in the keywords **"beginners celts"**. Make sure you ask a grown-up before going online.

Notes for grown-ups

Please read the internet safety guidelines at Usborne Quicklinks with your child. Children should be supervised online. The websites are regularly reviewed and the links at Usborne Quicklinks are updated. However, Usborne Publishing is not responsible and does not accept liability for the content or availability of any website other than its own.

A broken Celtic carnyx was found in Scotland. This is what it would have looked like when it was made. The top is shaped like a boar's head.

Index

bards, 4, 22-23, 30
Boudica, 26
carnyxes, 20, 30, 31
chariots, 21, 28, 30
crops, 5, 10
druids, 4, 16-17, 30
dye, 12, 20, 30
Europe, 3, 24
feasts, 18, 22
festivals, 18-19
gods and goddesses, 16, 18, 28, 29
hillforts, 6-7, 8, 30
Iron Age, 3
Romans, 24, 25, 26, 27, 28
round houses, 8-9
tools, 3, 10, 16
torcs, 13, 30
tribes, 4-5, 6, 7, 20, 24, 25, 26
Vercingetorix, 25
warriors, 4, 20-21, 22, 23, 30
weapons, 3, 16, 21, 28
woad, 20, 30

Acknowledgements

Photographic manipulation by John Russell

Photo credits

The publishers are grateful to the following for permission to reproduce material: **cover** © Heritage Image Partnership Ltd/Alamy; **p01** © C M Dixon/Heritage Images; **p06-07** © Jason Hawkes/CORBIS; **p10-11** © Trustees of the British Museum; **p12-13** © Trustees of the British Museum; **p14-15** © akg-images/Erich Lessing; **p16-17** © Chris Lisle/Corbis; **p22-23** © Mary Evans Picture Library/Alamy; **p24-25** © R. Sheridan/Ancient Art and Architecture Collection Ltd; **p26-27** © Robert Harding Picture Library/Alamy; **p28-29** © Heritage Images; **p30-31** © National Museums of Scotland.

Every effort has been made to trace and acknowledge ownership of copyright. If any rights have been omitted, the publishers offer to rectify this in any subsequent editions following notification.

This edition first published in 2020 by Usborne Publishing Ltd., Usborne House, 83-85 Saffron Hill, London EC1N 8RT, England. usborne.com Copyright © 2020, 2015, 2007 Usborne Publishing Ltd. All rights reserved. The name Usborne and the Balloon logo are Trade Marks of Usborne Publishing Ltd. No part of this publication may be reproduced, stored in a retrieval system, or transmitted in any form or by any means without the prior permission of Usborne Publishing Ltd. U.E.

The Stone Age

Jerome Martin

Illustrated by Colin King and Kimberley Scott
Designed by Amy Manning and Sam Whibley

Stone Age expert: Dr. Caroline McDonald, Museum of London
Reading consultant: Alison Kelly

Contents

 3 Long, long ago
 4 On the move
 6 Stone tools
 8 Hunting animals
10 Fishing
12 Gathering food
14 Making clothes
16 Stone Age homes
18 Cave painters
20 Carving
22 The first farmers
24 Building houses
26 Standing stones
28 How do we know?
30 Glossary
31 Usborne Quicklinks
32 Index

Long, long ago

The Stone Age began a very, very long time ago, when the first people started making tools from stone.

It lasted until around 4,000 years ago.

Stone Age people also made tools from other natural things such as wood, bone, animal skins, deer antlers and plants.

On the move

For most of the Stone Age, people found food by gathering wild plants and hunting wild animals.

They lived in small groups. Each group moved from place to place to find enough food.

Sometimes dogs helped people to carry things.

People built simple shelters to sleep in.

They made fires for cooking food and keeping warm.

Tame dogs helped with hunting.

Stone tools

People made many different types of tools out of stone.

Hand axes were made for cutting meat or plants.

Arrows for hunting were made with stone tips.

Scrapers were used to clean animal skins for making clothes.

Good tool makers were very important people. They sat in the warmest spot near the fire.

Each stone tool had to be hammered and chipped into shape. It was very hard work.

First, a tool maker chose a stone of the right type, shape and size.

Next, she used an even harder stone to hammer off big pieces.

Finally, she used an antler to chip off small flakes and make a sharp edge.

Hunting animals

People hunted wild animals for their meat.

Some hunters used fire to chase groups of bison until they fell over cliffs.

Other hunters trapped reindeer in narrow valleys. They threw spears at them.

People often used bows and arrows to shoot small animals and birds.

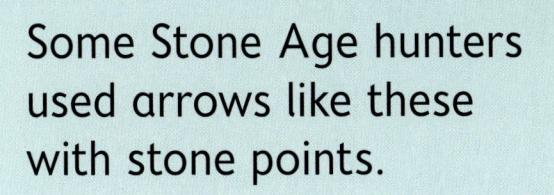

Some Stone Age hunters used arrows like these with stone points.

The points were attached to sticks using glue and string made from animal parts.

Feathers helped the arrows to fly straight.

In the Stone Age, both men and women went hunting.

Fishing

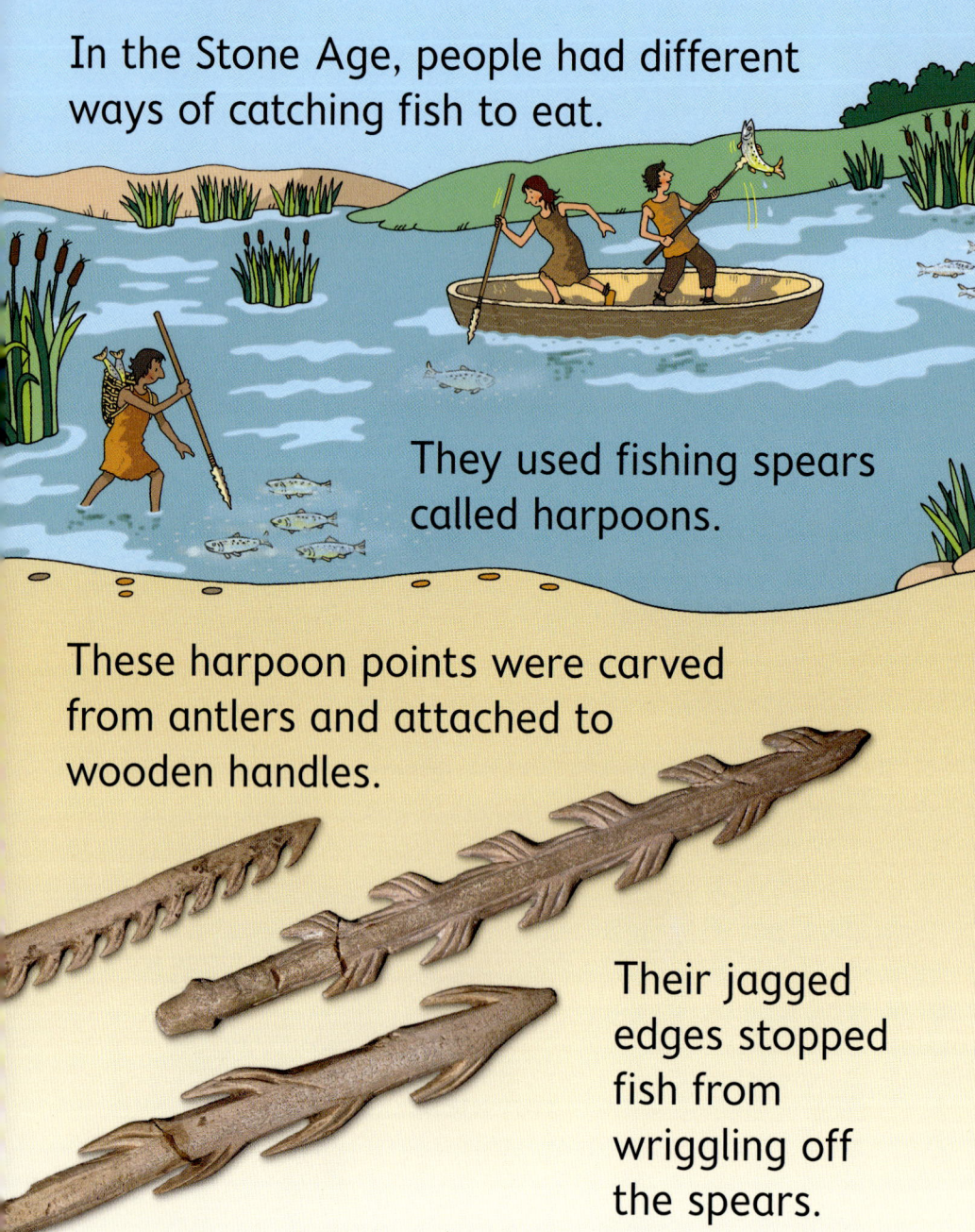

In the Stone Age, people had different ways of catching fish to eat.

They used fishing spears called harpoons.

These harpoon points were carved from antlers and attached to wooden handles.

Their jagged edges stopped fish from wriggling off the spears.

They also used fish hooks made from bone, and fishing lines and nets made from twisted grass.

Stone Age people also invented clever traps for catching fish.

They blocked a fast-flowing stream with stones and a woven basket.

The water swept through holes in the basket while the fish got stuck inside.

Gathering food

Stone Age people didn't just hunt animals for food. They gathered wild food such as roots, berries, nuts and seeds.

Collecting honey

Knocking down nuts

Gathering berries

Gathering seeds

Digging up roots

Picking water plants

They made a type of bread from the seeds of barley or wheat.

First, they used stones to crush the seeds into a powder.

Then they mixed the powder with water to make dough.

They baked the dough on flat rocks placed on a fire.

Grinding seeds took hours, and gave people very sore backs.

Oww!

Making clothes

Clothes were often made from the skins of animals such as deer.

People scraped the skins clean and then rubbed them until they were soft.

The skins were cut into pieces and holes were made in the edges with a stone tool.

The pieces were stitched into warm clothes using needles made from bone.

People also wore
necklaces and bracelets like these.

They made the beads from shells, bones,
animal teeth and pebbles.

Sometimes sea shells were sewn
onto clothes for decoration.

Stone Age homes

People made different types of shelters, using whatever they could find nearby.

Huts were built using branches and lots of thick bundles of dry reeds.

Some people lived in caves. They blocked part of the entrance to keep out the wind.

Other people made homes from the bones and skins of huge animals called mammoths.

This is what a Stone Age hut might have looked like.

It is made from branches covered in soil and grass.

Cave painters

Stone Age people painted on the walls of caves.

This painting from a cave in France shows a type of horse.

For paint, people crushed up yellow or red rocks, or black soot from the fire.

Then they mixed the powder with spit or with sticky animal fat.

They used their fingers, or brushes made of twigs, hair, moss or feathers.

Sometimes they made shapes by blowing paint over their hands.

Carving

Stone Age people also made elegant carvings from bones, antlers and tusks.

These pieces of reindeer antler are carved with curly patterns.

This carving of a woman's head was made from mammoth tusk.

Carving wasn't easy. It took lots of time.

First, the artist cut out a rough shape using a blade made from stone.

The shape was rubbed with fine sand and animal skin to smooth it.

A stone tool with a sharp point was used to carve fine lines and patterns.

People also carved flutes and whistles from hollow bird bones.

The first farmers

Some people discovered how to grow crops and raise animals for food. This is how the first farms started.

At first, people collected seeds from wild plants, and caught wild animals.

Then, they learned how to grow plants from the seeds and tame the animals.

Some farmers went to new places to find more land. Farming spread all over the world.

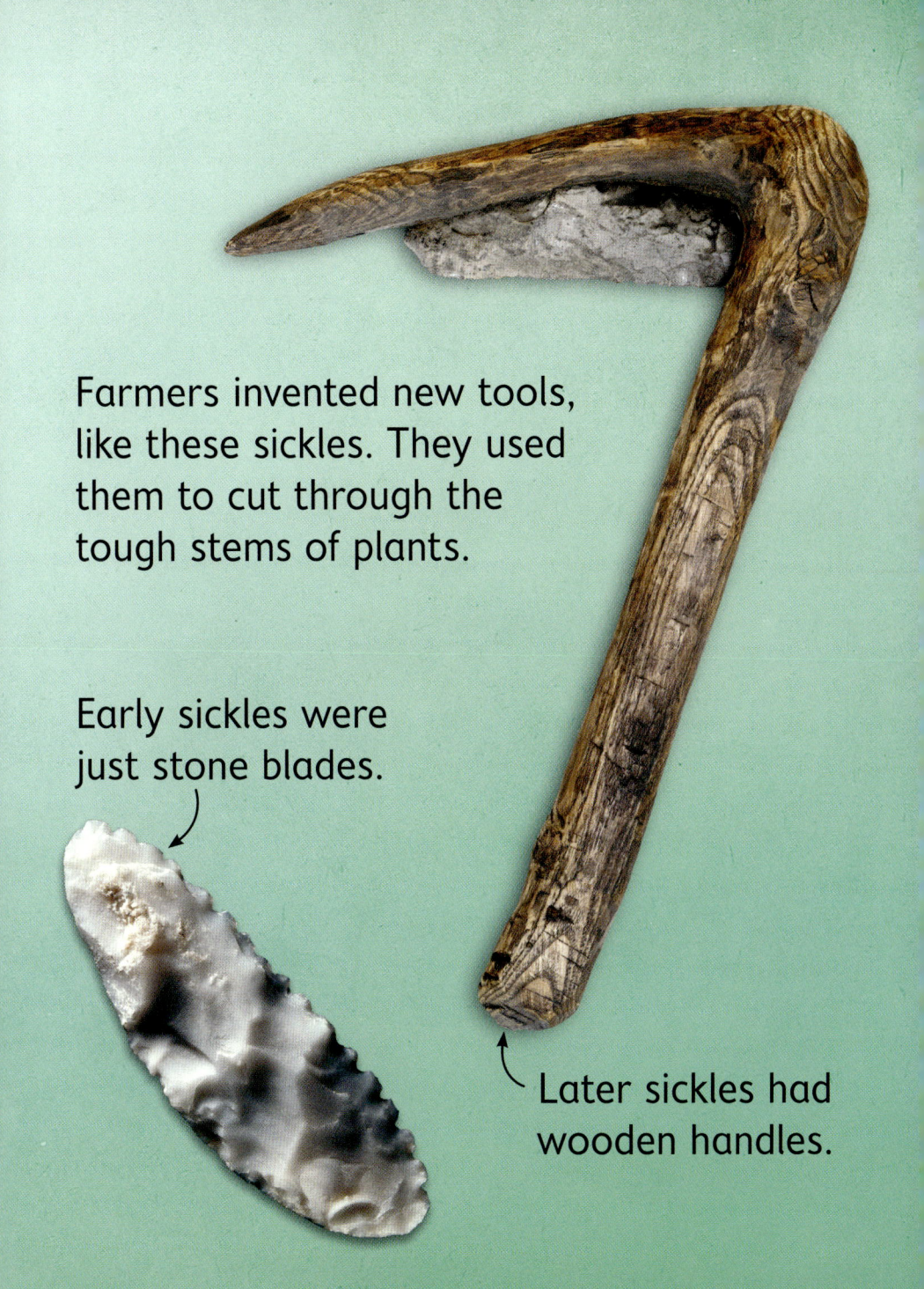

Farmers invented new tools, like these sickles. They used them to cut through the tough stems of plants.

Early sickles were just stone blades.

Later sickles had wooden handles.

Building houses

Now people were farming, they didn't need to keep moving around to find food. They stayed in one place.

They cut down trees to make fields and built big, strong houses to live in.

More and more people built fields and houses. These were the first villages.

People started making pots from baked clay. They used them for cooking and storing food.

These pots are from Sweden.

They are over 4,000 years old.

People often decorated pots by pressing shells or twisted rope into the wet clay.

Standing stones

At the end of the Stone Age, people built monuments using huge stones.

This famous monument is called Stonehenge. It's in England.

These huge stones were put up around 4,500 years ago.

Some of them have other stones lying on top of them.

The stones around the outside once formed a circle, but some of them have fallen over.

No one knows exactly what monuments like this were for.

How do we know?

Some Stone Age things have survived for thousands of years, buried in the ground or frozen in ice. Experts dig them up to find out more about life in the Stone Age.

This Stone Age home is 5,000 years old. It had a roof when people lived there.

Shelves

Entrance

Fireplace

Experts learn about Stone Age people by studying their bones and their tools.

Carvings and cave paintings teach them about early art, animals and hunting.

Some experts learn even more by living like Stone Age people.

Glossary

Here are some of the words in this book you might not know. This page tells you what they mean.

antlers - bony spikes that grow from the heads of deer.

bison - a large animal like a cow with a shaggy mane and a hump.

harpoon - a spear with a jagged point, used for hunting fish.

mammoth - an elephant-like animal with tusks that lived long ago.

blade - a tool (or part of a tool) used for cutting.

sickle - a curved tool with a sharp edge used for cutting plants.

monument - a group of huge stones, often set up in a line or circle.

Usborne Quicklinks

Would you like to find out more about the Stone Age? You can visit Usborne Quicklinks for links to websites with videos, amazing facts and things to make and do.

Go to **usborne.com/Quicklinks** and type in the keywords "**beginners Stone Age**".
Make sure you ask a grown-up before going online.

Notes for grown-ups

Please read the internet safety guidelines at Usborne Quicklinks with your child. Children should be supervised online. The websites are regularly reviewed and the links at Usborne Quicklinks are updated. However, Usborne Publishing is not responsible and does not accept liability for the content or availability of any website other than its own.

This bison is carved from a reindeer antler. It's around 15,000 years old.

Index

antlers, 3, 7, 10, 20, 30, 31
arrows, 6, 8, 9
bison, 8, 30, 31
blades, 21, 23, 30
bones, 3, 11, 14, 15, 16, 20-21, 29
carving, 10, 20-21, 29
caves, 16, 18-19, 29
clothes, 6, 14-15
cooking, 5, 13, 25
farming, 22-23, 24
fire, 5, 6, 8, 13, 19, 28
fishing, 10-11
food, 4, 5, 8-9, 10-11, 12-13, 22, 24, 25

harpoons, 10, 30
homes, 16-17, 24, 28
hunting, 4, 5, 6, 8-9, 12, 29
mammoths, 16, 20, 30
monuments, 26-27, 30
painting, 18-19, 29
seeds, 12, 13, 22
shells, 15, 25
shelters, 5, 16-17, 24, 28
sickles, 23, 30
skins, 3, 6, 14, 16
spears, 8, 10
Stonehenge, 26-27
tools, 3, 6-7, 14, 21, 23, 29
tusks, 20, 30

Acknowledgments

Photographic manipulation by John Russell
Picture research by Ruth King

Photo credits

The publishers are grateful to the following for permission to reproduce material:
Cover © Jean-Daniel Sudres/Hemis/Corbis; **p1** © Martin Zwick/age fotostock/Superstock; **p6** (top) © The Trustees of the British Museum; (middle) © De Agostini/N. Cirani/Getty Images; (bottom) © The Trustees of the Natural History Museum, London; **p9** © DTaggart84319/iStock; **p10** © RMN-Grand Palais (musée d'Archéologie nationale)/Jean Schormans; **p15** © RMN-Grand Palais (musée d'Archéologie nationale)/Jean Schormans; **p17** © Peter Howard; **p18** © Glasshouse Images/Alamy; **p20** (top) © RMN-Grand Palais (musée d'Archéologie nationale)/Loïc Hamon; (bottom) © RMN-Grand Palais (musée d'Archéologie nationale)/Jean-Gilles Berizzi; **p23** (top) © Museum of London; (bottom) © Album/ASF/Album alb2106827/Superstock; **p25** © DEA/G. Dagli Orti/Getty Images; **p26-27** © Jason Hawkes/Getty Images; **p28-29** © Worldwide Picture Library/Alamy; **p31** © Hervé Champollion/akg-images.

Every effort has been made to trace and acknowledge ownership of copyright. If any rights have been omitted, the publishers offer to rectify this in any subsequent editions following notification.

This edition first published in 2020 by Usborne Publishing Ltd., Usborne House, 83-85 Saffron Hill, London EC1N 8RT, England. usborne.com Copyright © 2020, 2015 Usborne Publishing Ltd. All rights reserved. The name Usborne and the Balloon logo are Trade Marks of Usborne Publishing Ltd. No part of this publication may be reproduced, stored in a retrieval system, or transmitted in any form or by any means without the prior permission of Usborne Publishing Ltd. U.E.

The Iron Age

Emily Bone

Illustrated by Colin King
Additional illustrations by Kimberley Scott
Designed by Alice Reese

Iron Age expert: Dr. Anne Millard
Reading consultant: Alison Kelly

Contents

- 3 A new discovery
- 4 Made of iron
- 6 How was it made?
- 8 Living in tribes
- 10 At home
- 12 On the farm
- 14 Living on a hill
- 16 Dressing up
- 18 Fun festivals
- 20 Iron Age gods
- 22 An Iron Age funeral
- 24 Iron Age warriors
- 26 Words and pictures
- 28 How do we know?
- 30 Glossary
- 31 Usborne Quicklinks
- 32 Index

A new discovery

Nearly 3,000 years ago, people discovered a metal called iron. This was the start of a time known as the Iron Age.

This is an iron ornament called a firedog. A wealthy Iron Age family used it to decorate the fireplace in their home.

Made of iron

Iron was strong. People used it to make tools, cooking pots and weapons.

Iron tools were used to dig up the ground and plant crops.

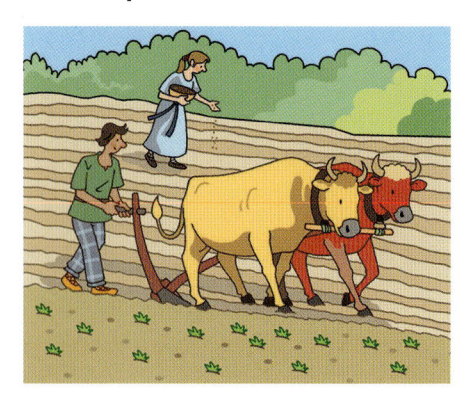

People cooked food over their fires in iron pots.

Horses had iron and leather harnesses to pull carts.

Weapons were made with iron blades.

This is an Iron Age dagger from Spain. Its blade has an iron cover called a scabbard.

Part of the scabbard is missing. This is because very old iron rusts away.

How was it made?

Most iron was made in a very hot oven called a furnace. A metalworker then shaped the iron. This is how a sword was made.

To make the furnace very hot, air was blown into it using tools called bellows.

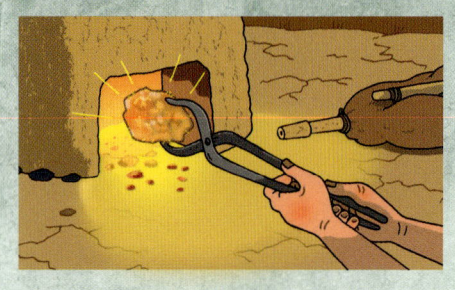

A rock called iron ore was put into the furnace. Heating the rock made iron.

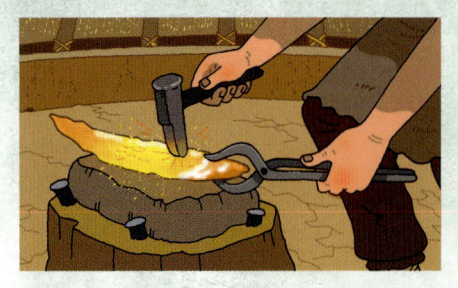

The metalworker used a hammer to shape the hot iron into a sword.

Then, the metalworker plunged the sword into cold water to make it stronger.

People decorated iron things with glass and other metals.

These are parts of a horse's harness. The patterns are made from stained glass and copper.

Living in tribes

Most Iron Age people lived in groups called tribes. Different people in a tribe did different things.

Chiefs made sure people followed the rules of the tribe.

People came to a priest or priestess for advice.

Men in each tribe trained to be fearsome warriors.

Most people were farmers, growing food and raising animals.

Metalworkers were very important people in a tribe.

They made things from iron and other metals, such as bronze, copper, gold and silver. This is a bronze ornament of a bull.

At home

Tribes built houses from materials that they found nearby.

Brochs were tall, stone towers with four floors and lots of rooms.

A longhouse had a long, sloping roof. Animals were kept in part of the house.

Crannogs were built on top of wooden posts over lakes.

Many tribes built roundhouses, like this one. Part of it has been cut away so you can see inside.

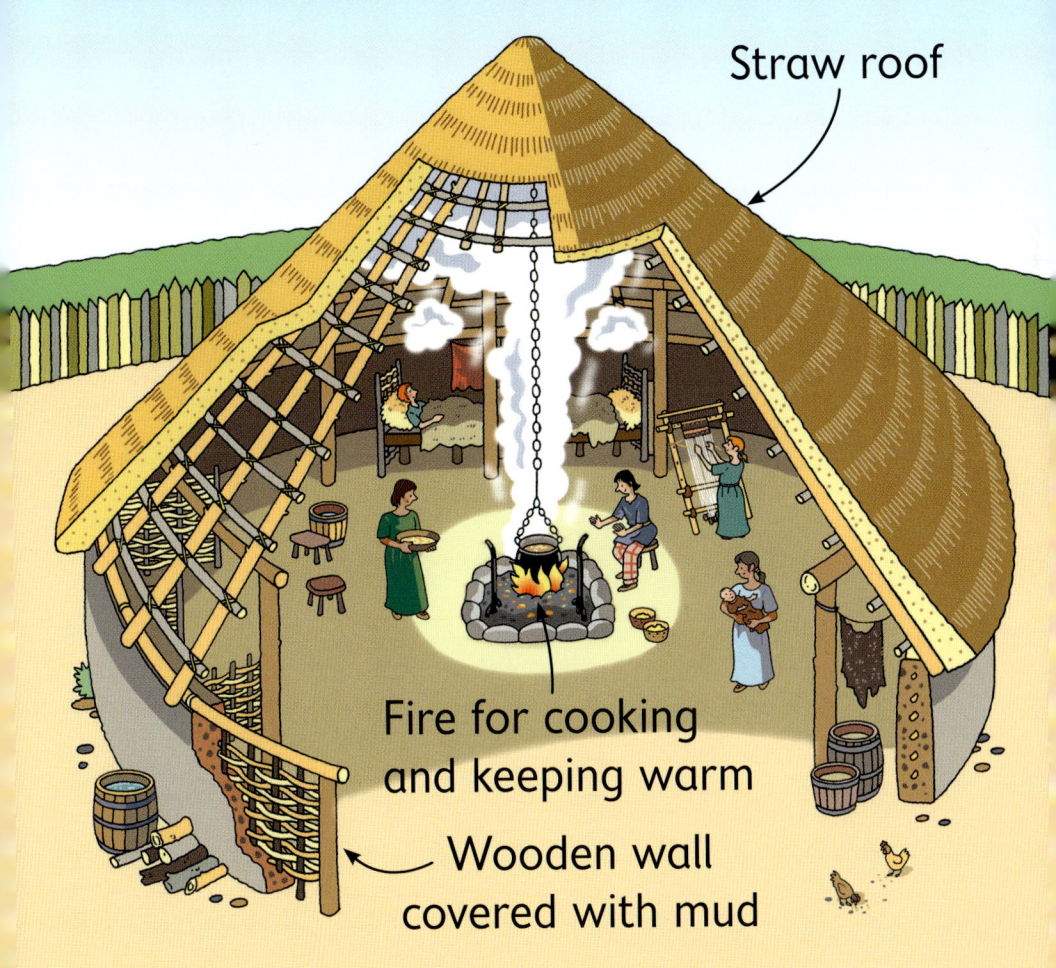

Straw roof

Fire for cooking and keeping warm

Wooden wall covered with mud

A family cooked, ate and slept in one big room.

On the farm

Most Iron Age people lived on small farms.

Farmers grew wheat in fields and cut it down using iron tools called sickles.

They ground the wheat into flour, then used it to make bread.

Farmers also had to look after the animals they kept on their farms.

They milked the cows, goats or sheep, then made the milk into cheese.

Trees were cut down
to build houses.

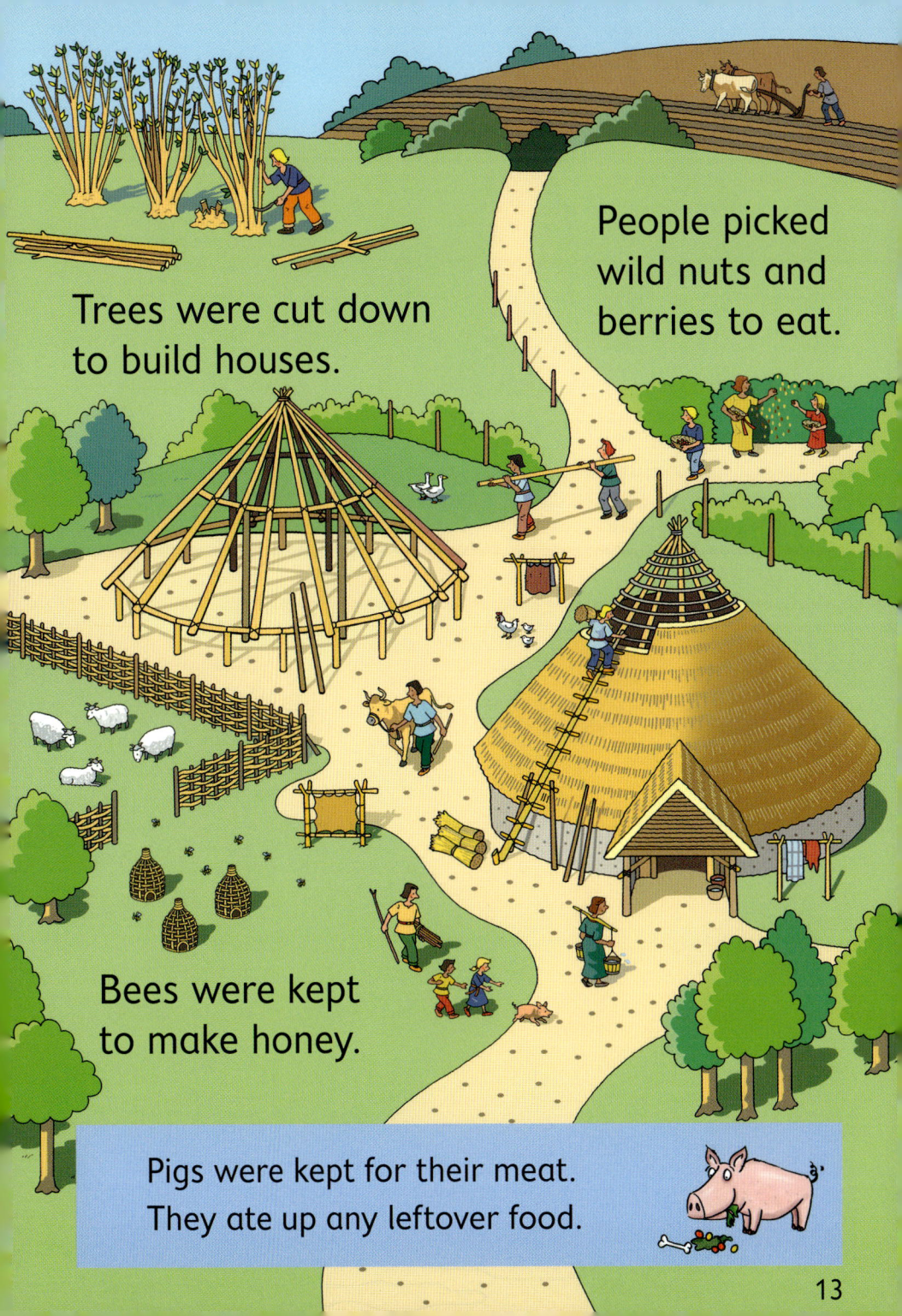

People picked
wild nuts and
berries to eat.

Bees were kept
to make honey.

Pigs were kept for their meat.
They ate up any leftover food.

Living on a hill

Many tribes were attacked by other tribes who wanted to steal from them.

Some tribes built forts with steep banks on the tops of high hills to stay safe. These forts also showed how powerful they were.

The fort was in here.

Here are the remains of a big Iron Age hillfort called Maiden Castle in the south of England.

From the hillfort, an attacking tribe could be seen from a long way away.

Ditches and steep banks made it difficult for attackers to climb the hill.

There were only one or two entrances. These could be shut off by heavy gates.

The tribe inside the fort threw rocks and spears over the tall, wooden walls.

Dressing up

Iron Age women made clothes.

They used plants to dye wool. Then, they wove the wool into cloth.

Men wore long shirts with baggy leggings. Women wore long dresses.

Warm cloaks made from sheepskin or wool were held in place with a brooch.

For special occasions, people put on metal bracelets and necklaces.

This is a type of necklace called a torc.

It is made from gold. Gold was very expensive, so only a rich Iron Age person would have worn it.

Iron Age people let their hair grow long and liked to try out different styles.

Fun festivals

Throughout the year, Iron Age people held many festivals. Here are some of them.

People lit fires to celebrate the first lambs being born.

Men had horse racing contests at summer festivals.

At spring festivals, cows and sheep were made to run between two fires.

People hoped that this would keep the animals safe for the coming year.

At many festivals, there were huge fires and feasts. People cooked food in big pots called cauldrons.

This cauldron, from Ireland, was probably used to cook meat stews.

At one festival, people believed that the dead came back to see their friends and families.

Iron Age gods

Iron Age people believed in many gods. They gave presents to the gods to try and keep them happy.

Priests placed gifts of necklaces and weapons into a river for the gods to find.

People made statues of the gods in the forest and put gifts next to them.

Farmers left gifts around their houses and fields for the gods, too.

This valuable silver pot is called the Gundestrup Cauldron. It was found in a bog where it had been buried as a gift.

The pictures on the cauldron are probably of different gods.

Sometimes, people or animals were killed to give as gifts.

An Iron Age funeral

Sometimes, when a very important person died, they were given a big funeral.

A dead priestess was laid on a chariot she owned when she was alive.

Members of her tribe had a big feast.

They took the body to a grave. Then, they laid the body in it.

Food and things that the priestess owned were placed next to her.

The chariot was taken apart and placed in the grave, too. Everything was covered with a mound of earth.

Iron Age warriors

Young and fit men were fierce warriors. They defended their homes from attack. Sometimes, women were warriors, too.

Warriors charged at their enemies with iron swords or spears.

They used wooden shields to protect themselves.

Some warriors wore helmets, too.

Warriors blew trumpets, called carnyxes. These made a loud noise to scare the enemy.

Some rode on chariots.

Warriors jumped off to fight, then jumped back on.

Some warriors painted their bodies with dye and spiked their hair to look more frightening.

Words and pictures

Many Iron Age people didn't know how to read or write. Each tribe had its own bard to tell people important things.

Usually, the bard would play an instrument and sing.

He sang songs making fun of the chief's enemies.

The bard would tell everyone if the tribe won a battle.

He also sang stories about the history of the tribe.

Pictures told people different things, too.

This is a coin with a picture of someone riding a horse.

Horses were a sign of power. The people who made the coin were showing that their tribe were fearsome warriors.

How do we know?

We know about the lives of Iron Age people because experts have found and studied the things they used to own.

At a hillfort, experts remove the top layer of soil.

Very carefully, they dig into the soil until they find something.

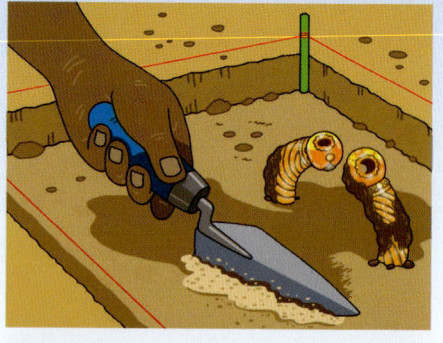

They brush off the soil, then take the item away to study it.

Experts have found whole bodies of Iron Age people.

This man was found in a bog in Denmark.

He died over 2,000 years ago but the mud has stopped his body from rotting away.

Glossary

Here are some of the words in this book you might not know. This page tells you what they mean.

iron - a strong, hard metal that can be used to make many things.

furnace - a type of oven used to make iron.

bellows - tools to blow air into a furnace and make it very hot.

tribe - Iron Age people who lived in the same area and did similar things.

roundhouse - a type of house that some Iron Age people lived in.

hillfort - forts built by tribes on hills to help them stay safe.

bard - a storyteller and singer in a tribe who passed on information.

Usborne Quicklinks

Would you like to find out more about the Iron Age? You can visit Usborne Quicklinks for links to websites with videos, amazing facts and things to make and do.

Go to **usborne.com/Quicklinks** and type in the keywords "**beginners Iron Age**". Make sure you ask a grown-up before going online.

Notes for grown-ups

Please read the internet safety guidelines at Usborne Quicklinks with your child. Children should be supervised online. The websites are regularly reviewed and the links at Usborne Quicklinks are updated. However, Usborne Publishing is not responsible and does not accept liability for the content or availability of any website other than its own.

This is a statue of an Iron Age god found in the Czech Republic. People left gifts for the god around it.

Index

animals, 4, 10, 12, 13, 18, 27
bards, 26, 30
bellows, 6, 30
bogs, 21, 29
chariots, 22, 23, 25
chiefs, 8, 26
clothing, 16-17
cooking, 4, 11, 19
farming, 4, 8, 12-13
festivals, 18-19
food, 4, 12, 13, 19, 22, 23
funerals, 22-23
furnaces, 6, 30
gods, 20-21, 31
harnesses, 4, 7

hillforts, 14-15, 28, 30
houses, 10-11, 13, 30
iron, 3, 4-5, 6-7, 9, 12, 24, 30
metalworkers, 6, 9
ornaments, 2-3, 9
pictures, 21, 27
pots, 4, 19, 21
priests, 8, 20, 22, 23
roundhouses, 11, 13, 30
studying, 28-29
tools, 4, 6, 12
torcs, 17
tribes, 8-9, 14, 15, 26, 27, 30
warriors, 8, 24-25, 27
weapons, 5, 6, 15, 20, 24, 25

Acknowledgments

Photographic manipulation by John Russell
Picture research by Ruth King
Additional design by Helen Edmonds

Photo credits

The publishers are grateful to the following for permission to reproduce material: **cover** © Heritage Image Partnership Ltd/Alamy (detail from the Gundestrup Cauldron); **p1** © Peter Carroll/Alamy (an Iron Age crannog house in Scotland, U.K.); **p2-3** © Amgueddfa Cymru – National Museum Wales; **p5** © Dagger, Halstatt Culture, c.750-450 BC (iron), Iron Age/Musée des Antiquités Nationales, St. Germain-en-Laye, France/Bridgeman Images; **p7** © The Trustees of the British Museum; **p9** © Cast of a small bull figurine found in a cave of the Moravian Karst/Werner Forman Archive/Bridgeman Images; **p14** © Robert Harding Picture Library Ltd/Alamy; **p17** © The Trustees of the British Museum; **p19** © The Trustees of the British Museum; **p21** © INTERFOT/Alamy; **p27** © Celtic coin of horse and rider/Werner Forman Archive/Bridgeman Images; **p29** © Heritage Image Partnership Ltd/Alamy; **p31** © God's Head, from the Sanctuary of Msecke Zebrovice, Bohemia (stone)/Bridgeman Images.

Every effort has been made to trace and acknowledge ownership of copyright. If any rights have been omitted, the publishers offer to rectify this in any subsequent editions following notification.

This edition first published in 2021 by Usborne Publishing Ltd., Usborne House, 83-85 Saffron Hill, London EC1N 8RT, England. usborne.com Copyright © 2021, 2015 Usborne Publishing Ltd. All rights reserved. The name Usborne and the Balloon logo are Trade Marks of Usborne Publishing Ltd. No part of this publication may be reproduced, stored in a retrieval system, or transmitted in any form or by any means without the prior permission of Usborne Publishing Ltd. U.E.